## Praise for *Worst Enemy, Best Teacher*

"For years I have heard (and taught) that our greatest challenges are our greatest teachers. Finally, *Worst Enemy, Best Teacher* is the book that gives one the skills to make that happen. With specific stories and tools, Dr. Combs provides the reader with a unique resource for turning the worst that can come our way into possibly the best."

— David Baum, PhD, D.Min., author of *Lightning in a Bottle: Proven Lessons for Leading Change* and *The Randori Principles: The Path of Effortless Leadership*

"Deidre Combs offers readers specific, easy-to-use strategies for becoming effective leaders in the face of conflict and confrontation. She challenges us to recognize opponents and transform our relationships with them, allowing us to move toward a greater sense of wholeness, equilibrium, and peace."

— Nancy Nelson, PhD, professor of adolescent psychology, Edgewood College, Madison, Wisconsin

"Written with remarkable insight and candor, *Worst Enemy, Best Teacher* offers us the courage and the tools to confront some of life's most daunting challenges. Combs deals frankly and optimistically with the issues that send most of us running for cover, convincingly making the argument that it is precisely those people who drive us crazy, our most intractable opponents, who will be our best teachers if we are prepared to engage them. I finished this book inspired and ready to take up the battle with optimism and a heart open to change."

— Marcus Stevens, author of *The Curve of the World* and *Useful Girl*

"With diverse references, inspiring real-life examples, and practical, easy-to-employ exercises, Deidre Combs's powerful book *Worst Enemy, Best Teacher* offers a wealth of important resources for living in our pluralistic world. With compassion and insight, Combs invites her readers to see interpersonal conflicts as opportunities holding great gifts of wisdom and understanding — a philosophy that will bring healing not only to individual lives but to our world as well."

— Maggie Oman Shannon, author of *The Way We Pray* and *One God, Shared Hope*

# WORST ENEMY BEST TEACHER

# WORST ENEMY BEST TEACHER

HOW TO SURVIVE AND THRIVE WITH OPPONENTS, COMPETITORS, AND THE PEOPLE WHO DRIVE YOU CRAZY

DEIDRE COMBS

JAICO PUBLISHING HOUSE

Ahmedabad Bangalore Bhopal Bhubaneswar Chennai
Delhi Hyderabad Kolkata Lucknow Mumbai

Published by Jaico Publishing House
A-2 Jash Chambers, 7-A Sir Phirozshah Mehta Road
Fort, Mumbai - 400 001
jaicopub@jaicobooks.com
www.jaicobooks.com



Published in arrangement with
New World Library
a division of Whatever Publishing Inc.
14 Pamaron Way, Novato, CA 94949, USA

To be sold only in India, Bangladesh, Bhutan,
Pakistan, Nepal, Sri Lanka and the Maldives.

WORST ENEMY, BEST TEACHER
ISBN 978-93-86867-77-3

First Jaico Impression: 2018
Fifth Jaico Impression: 2019



Printed by
Repro India Limited
Plot No. 50/2, T.T.C. MIDC Industrial Area
Mahape, Navi Mumbai - 400 710

*For Cameron, Cody, and Senya*

*We are continually faced with great opportunities which are brilliantly disguised as unsolvable problems.*

— MARGARET MEAD

# Contents

# Introduction

*One must think like a hero*
*to behave like a merely decent human being.*

— MAY SARTON

There's no getting around it: there will be people in our lives who simply drive us crazy. Call them what you will — enemy, competitor, or in-law — they can get under your skin and make your life miserable. They "stick in your craw," as my Western neighbors like to say.

There is the "everything about you makes me see red" category: the coworker who is always sucking up to the boss, the politician whose policies you find repugnant, the parent who turns Thanksgiving dinners into episodes of the political TV talk show *Hardball*, or the celebrity-turned-activist on the morning news program.

And then there is the "if only you didn't have that one annoying quirk" group: the assistant who snaps his gum, the sibling who says inappropriate things in movie theatres, the friend who requires daily pep talks, or the spouse who plays "let's talk about disturbing items from today's news" just before you go to sleep (a real-life example).

For the most part, we try to grin and bear it and work around these people and their annoyances as a part of life, much like disease, aging, and embarrassing skin blemishes. But that doesn't stop us from periodically pausing to stroke our chins, gaze upward, and fantasize: *"Hmmmm, wouldn't life be grand if Joe just wasn't a part of it?"*

But unlike that ratty couch from your college days, or that plaid skirt that has fallen out of fashion, you can't just donate these people to Goodwill. Nor is simply ignoring them an option: his smiling mug frequents the front page of the daily newspaper, or her office is just across the hall. Sure, you might be able to fire or run away from a particular pesky troublemaker, but another just like him will inevitably take his place. Most bothersome of all, sometimes these folks are our relatives! With each visit or phone call, they will remind us of the misery they can bestow and the control they can have on our lives.

> *In order to have an enemy, one must be somebody. One must be a force before he can be resisted by another force. A malicious enemy is better than a clumsy friend.*
>
> — ANNE SOPHIE SWETCHINE

Short of living as a hermit, is there a way to deal with these crazy-makers? Is there a way to not only cope with these folks but view them as a means to self-knowledge and improvement? To not just tolerate them but learn to actually *appreciate* them?

The answer is "yes!" And you are about to learn how. We do not have to like our foes, and we may justly fear them, but we can improve through their presence. Enemies can bring new insight and opportunities. We can respond smartly to our adversaries and move beyond the annoyances and threats. Conflict can actually expand our awareness and clarify our priorities so that we emerge from its chaos wiser, better prepared, and in a much happier state of mind.

When we use a conflict to improve ourselves, rather than running away or ignoring our opponent, we embark on an archetypal *warrior's* path. Over thousands of years, heroic warriors were vigorously conditioned to respond effectively under stress and to learn from their adversaries. And, as described in the myths of Camelot from the British Isles, the Asian martial arts, and the Native American traditions, these warriors were trained to use their resulting knowledge responsibly, to treat others well, and to live by a clear code of conduct. Instead of being victims, they strove to honestly accept their circumstances and improve them. As a result, these combatants became confident, strong, and successful.

> *There is in the worst of fortunes the best of chances for a happy change.*
>
> — EURIPIDES

Unfortunately, some holding the warrior title have not valued their opponents nor used their power admirably. Self-serving desires often eclipse a warrior's integrity. This failure of responsibility has ravaged families, organizations, and cultures. Military misconduct, corporate mismanagement, and other forms of abuse have made *warrior* a dirty word.

Yet the classical warrior's highest aim is not to vanquish the enemy and take the spoils of battle but to find a creative solution that serves all sides. Anyone who wishes to be courageous and astute when confronting great challenges or difficult people can draw from these skills. This book synthesizes ancient training techniques with recent brain research, other scientific findings, and cross-cultural spiritual teachings to create an *everyday warrior's* skill set.

For example, say you were bequeathed a challenging sister-in-law, Suzie, who loves to fill your email inbox with ludicrous political propaganda and inject her forceful opinions into every family conversation. After reading this book, when you find yourself in a room with Suzie, instead of trying to sneak out a back door, you can employ these everyday techniques to:

- Gather new, valuable information about the dispute
- Learn more about yourself
- Strengthen your capabilities
- Develop a greater sense of inner peace

These are the ultimate benefits, but there is a more immediate one as well: We can move beyond the conflict at hand and *neutralize* the toxic effect that Suzie has on us. The more we know, the better we can progress and the less she will bother us.

As we gain awareness, strength, and greater calm, these rewards not only transform the relationship in question but can improve our connections with everyone around us. We become more comfortable with adversity and bring new calm into our homes, communities, and workplaces. We simply find we have more room for others and ourselves.

Of course, it won't always be easy. Opponents knock us down. As everyday warriors we will endeavor to get back up and use what we have learned to better ourselves and potentially the greater world. Israeli Robi Damelin and Palestinian Nadwa Sarandah bravely fight to break down stereotypes and bring peace to their region. Yet, in 2002 Robi lost her twenty-eight-year-old son, David, to a Palestinian sniper and Nadwa's beloved sister Naila was stabbed to death on the street by a Jewish settler. Both women were initially devastated. "I would do anything to bring my sister back," says Nadwa. Robi adds, "Through this process one's sense of values can become sharpened, or they may die. For me, it became a fundamental choice to either stay a victim or find where I could make a difference. My choice gives me the strength to go on."

Meeting through a group of bereaved Israeli and Palestinian families, together Robi and Nadwa now traverse their region speaking to students and stricken parents to foster dialogue. "Sometimes I am the first Israeli a Palestinian has ever met," says Robi. "We are all the same. We share the same pain and our tears are the same color."

> *Hidden blessings inside suffering.... Breaks create openings that were not there before, and in that space grow the seeds for new creation.*
>
> — REBECCA WELLS

Through their own experience they have become guides for others in similar circumstances and show them alternatives to revenge or hopelessness. "The common people have the power," Nadwa says. "We have seen this in South Africa and in efforts around the world; people talking to people can create peace."

In part 1 of the book, "Learning to Live Fully," we prepare ourselves to fight well. Chapter 1 explains why and how to see our enemies as teachers. Then in chapters 2 and 3 we identify with whom we are fighting, both externally and internally. In chapter 4 we'll explore some of the benefits that come from following this path.

Sometimes just recognizing our opponent and his role as teacher can bring these gifts. As an everyday example, my top opponent-turned-teacher over the past few years is a man I'll call Robert. I had perceived Robert as my opposite when it came to approaching disputes. He was the ruthless litigator, while I held the part of the touchy-feely mediator. Robert played the role of the agnostic, while I applied multicultural spiritual precepts to dealing with challenges. He was considered tough and heartless as he took down his legal opponents, while I got to be the "sweet" mom.

We had mutual friends, were cordial at parties, and even had each other over to dinner. I always respected his extraordinary intellect but was perplexed by his apparent disdain of my ideals. I didn't see him as an opponent and wouldn't even admit to myself how troubled I was by him. I just thought he was closed off and felt simultaneous pity and nervousness around him.

> *Tomorrow hopes that we have learned something from yesterday.*
>
> — JOHN WAYNE

One day Robert admitted to my husband that I bothered him. His honesty instigated my own self-reflection. First, I was put off that he had deceived me by pretending to like me in public. "What a liar," I thought, adding that to my list of ills. But eventually I had to admit that I was just as dishonest, if not more. I didn't like him either.

Throughout the world we find depictions of gods and other mystical beings with two opposing faces on a single head. For example, the dual-faced Roman god, Janus (depicted below), from which "January" comes, was the keeper of gates and doorways. Janus connected the opposites and created safety as he watched over our past and the road ahead.

Reflecting, I thought of Janus and wondered, "If I perceived Robert as my perfect opposite, maybe the traits I don't like in him could instead be found *within me* to watch my back." So as I prepared to teach, I began to ask myself what Robert might think. Was my presentation too touchy-feely, too optimistic or naive? What was I missing? This opponent brought me to a better internal balance between idealism and pragmatism. He might be a great teacher, yet, to begin to learn, I first had to admit that Robert was a valuable opponent. I had to overcome my own limited perceptions of what was "good" and "right" before I could learn from this potential ally.

Part 2 of the book, "An Everyday Warrior's Handbook," provides concrete techniques to help us to engage with our opponents and thrive under stress. Conflict takes time. In chapter 5, we will first look at how to engage so that we can last over the long haul. In chapters 6 and 7, "Sharpen the Mind" and "Tune the Heart," we will discover daily disciplines to heighten our awareness and to help us respond honorably so that we can survive and serve as leaders. Then in chapter 8, we will explore how to deal with people like Suzie or Robert who get under our skin.

> *Nothing would more contribute to make a man wise than to have always an enemy in his view.*
>
> — LORD HALIFAX

This everyday warrior philosophy was well understood by a beloved family friend, Len Hirsch. A story goes that Len was selected to serve on President Carter's transition team in 1976. As the group set up shop, Len, by reputation and seniority, had his pick of well-appointed offices. Instead, he chose a small cubicle next to a large office that had been selected by another assignee who wanted Len off the team. When asked why, Len simply replied, "Always stay close to your enemy. From him you'll learn the most." Even though Len and his adversary soon became allies, Len believed that even as an enemy this man could help him.

Learning from our opponents is not particularly easy, especially when they might wish to take what we hold dear. Yet even then, they bring opportunity. One business owner explained that his toughest adversary, Bill, was an employee who had systematically stolen from him for years. "Bill was good. I couldn't ever prove what I suspected, and to this day I am not sure exactly how much he took. But while I figured out how to get rid of him, I observed his tactics and learned about our company's critical weaknesses. Bill was an excellent teacher and one that I was happy to see go!"

> *He who wants a rose must respect the thorn.*
>
> — PERSIAN PROVERB

The methods described in *Worst Enemy, Best Teacher* teach us to hold all our opponent's capabilities, including the destructive ones, in the highest regard so that we might discover how to emerge in one piece while we improve. I hope that this book supports you to learn from adversity with confidence. May it help you to turn terrible enemies into valuable teachers and creatively resolve vexing problems within our families, our organizations, and our society.

PART ONE

# Learning to Live Fully

*No pressure, no diamonds.*

— MARY CASE

CHAPTER ONE

# See Your Enemy as a Teacher

*Listen to your enemy, for God is talking.*

— JEWISH PROVERB

*In India, everything has a purpose. The tea and the tea grower, the yogi and the thief, the mother and the child: all have a purpose.*

*One clear and temperate day, a Brahman, or priest, was walking happily down a dusty road when he heard the most terrible weeping coming from under a large tree. The Brahman knew that it was his job to help even the most pitiful, so he ran over to the tree to find a tiger in a cage. "Help me, help me," cried the tiger. "They are going to make a rug out of me. Please release me from this cage."*

*"Well," thought the Brahman, "it is my purpose to help even the most pitiful, but this is a tiger. He might eat me."*

*"Please, oh please, help me," sobbed the tiger.*

*"If I let you go," said the Brahman, "do you promise not to eat me?"*

*"I won't eat you. Please hurry and let me out," replied the tiger.*

*So the Brahman opened the cage and the tiger leapt out, right on top of the Brahman!*

*"Thank you," said the tiger. "Now prepare to be eaten."*

*"Is there no gratitude, did you not promise to spare me?" asked the Brahman.*

*The tiger thought for a moment or two and replied, "Let us do this. Go ask the first three things that you see on the road ahead if I should eat you. If one says no, then go on your way; otherwise, return to your destiny."*

*So grimly down the road went the Brahman until he came to a pipal tree. When he told the tree his situation, the tree replied, "All my life people have come and used my branches to make whips and fires. I give shade and shelter, and I am given nothing in return. There is no gratitude; the tiger is your destiny, return to be eaten."*

*Next, he found an elephant with an iron chain and ring attached to his foot. The Brahman wept as he told the elephant about the tiger and asked if the tiger should eat him. The elephant replied, "I work from morning to night for my master. I am whipped and chained. There is no gratitude. Go prepare to be eaten."*

*The Brahman looked down in despair and spoke to the road beneath him. "You have heard my story. Doeth thou think the tiger should eat me?" The road quickly replied, "Holy man, I have listened to your story and ask you to remember that I am useful to all. Nevertheless, people trample on me and drop their garbage upon my back. Return to the tiger."*

*As the Brahman began to walk back to the tiger, he heard a voice from behind him say, "I just don't understand, you want to eat a tiger?"*

*The Brahman spun around to see a small jackal sitting in the middle of the road. "No," said the Brahman. "The tiger wants to eat me," and he told the jackal his tale.*

*"Very strange, you are very scrawny, and you don't eat meat. I just don't understand. Take me to this tiger," the jackal commanded. So, frustrated with the jackal, the Brahman accompanied him back to the tiger.*

*The tiger lay under the large tree, purring with contentment. "You have returned, as I knew you would. Now, prepare for your fate," he said.*

*The jackal replied, "Very confusing, very confusing, I just don't understand. You are going to let this man eat you?"*

*"No, you silly creature," the tiger gruffly answered. "I am going to eat the man," and he explained the situation and how it was his destiny to eat the Brahman.*

*"I just don't understand why you would let a man eat you. How did the man get into the cage? Very strange, very strange," said the jackal.*

*"I AM GOING TO EAT HIM," roared the tiger. "I was in the cage, you idiot, like this!"*

*As the tiger leapt back into the cage, the jackal shut the door saying, "Don't let the tiger out again." And he ran away.*

*In the future, the Brahman was a wiser man. He continued to serve the poor and help even the most pitiful. But he had learned. If nothing else, he had learned that even tiger cages serve a purpose.*

> *If you want to make enemies, try to change something.*
>
> — WOODROW WILSON

Like the Brahman, we too may walk down happy roads, basically content with our lot, when we are called to react to an adversary. "Tigers" appear in our homes, in our businesses, and at our national borders. They shake up our worlds and can threaten our very existence. We may hate them and see their presence as an injustice, but as we will discuss in this chapter, even enemies have a purpose.

*Enemy*, what a strong word. When I speak and consult on

conflict strategies and recommend that we should "learn from the enemy" or "appreciate the enemy," many believe that this advice applies to very few in their lives. Initially, they think of enemies as dangerous criminals or those whom they know hate and wish to destroy them. They relegate the word to international conflicts, fierce personal battles, and serious illnesses like cancer.

However, the etymology of the word *enemy* describes it as simply "not friend." It is one that "opposes the purposes or interests of another." An "enemy" can thus be anyone, or anything, that brings difference or discord into our lives. With this broadened definition, a terrorist is of course an enemy, but so are a dear next-door neighbor and his barking puppy. Both business clients and trusted employees who disagree with a new policy would fit this description. Family members who strike out in directions for which we are not prepared become surprise adversaries. Viruses and death are global enemies. And the list continues. . . .

The bad news is, using this definition, we are surrounded by enemies. Initially that can be quite a fear-inducing thought. However, our opponents can bring us information that we most need at this time, which they are drawn to share with us. We can therefore view all opponents as potential teachers. This expanded description makes the world our classroom, where we are encircled by those who assist in our evolution and transformation. In this view, an enemy becomes anything that causes us problems, be it a bothersome person, a strange culture, or a chronic illness, and, like any other difficulty with which we are faced, it can be perceived as one who brings opportunity.

> *Be grateful even for hardship, setbacks, and bad people. Dealing with such obstacles is an essential part of training in the Art of Peace.*
>
> — MORIHEI UESHIBA

"The Tiger and the Brahman" is a *Jataka*, or a Buddhist teaching tale, that describes a past life of the Buddha. I tell stories monthly at a local elementary school and like to recount this tale and its origins. So when I ask which character the kids think is the Buddha, they will initially yell out, "The Brahman!" When I smile and don't respond, soon after I'll hear, "The jackal!" No one ever guesses the tiger.

We may not like them, and we might justly fear them, but we absolutely need our opponents. Without up there is no down. Without black, we have no white. Without the tiger, there is no wise Brahman. Our adversaries show us who we are by holding up a contrasting side. As one client told me, "My mother-in-law has always been extremely critical because we don't attend church. I hated her attacks, yet she was just what I needed to explore my spiritual beliefs and to share my discoveries with my children."

Through our adversaries' pushing, we can more clearly perceive our own capabilities and innate values. A newly married Iraqi woman in her twenties, Intisar, was directing a women's relief organization in her country soon after the war in 2003. "We must stay small for now because of those who oppose our work," Intisar explained. Yet through these trials, she has resolved to persevere: "I tell my family that they should not mourn for me if I die. In the past, others were killed for no reason. What I am doing has meaning, and this makes the dangers worth confronting."

If we forget that our opponent is a potential teacher, we can become distracted by the question "Why me?" The Brahman gets stuck in the injustice of it all and almost perishes as a result. We might ask, "Why is he picking on me?" or, "Why did this happen to us?" Although we can gather information with these queries so that the situation won't happen again, we won't learn anything until we accept our reality. As the elephant, tree, and road describe, life isn't always fair. Tigers eat people, terrorists bomb buildings, and illnesses attack our immune systems. These events are indeed horrible, but we need to accept what is and figure out what to do next.

> *An unencumbered stream has no song.*
>
> — ZEN SAYING

Jerry White, cofounder and president of Landmine Survivors Network, explains, "You probably remember a date that cleaved your personal history into 'before' and 'after.' [Landmine] survivors aren't the only ones who have devastating experiences. All of us have 'explosive' events — illnesses, deaths, accidents — that create an urgent need for resiliency and resolve. And each of us, if we're fortunate, may also have a day when we start to conquer those events."

We might also mistakenly believe that we already hold all the answers. The Brahman might have said, "It is my job to help even the most pitiful, and I know exactly what that means." Fixed perceptions leave us vulnerable, and we do not see other perspectives when we are sure we have the complete picture. With rigid views, we instead unconsciously invite opponents to drop by and show us what we have missed.

To learn from our opponent and to resolve conflict, we must change the paradigm. Conflict calls us to see the world in completely new ways. "So you want to eat a tiger?" Stand on your head and turn your beliefs inside out to see more broadly; from that perspective lies the true solution. Our dumb jackal was the wisest in the bunch. We must remember that nothing is fully as it seems.

In some conflicts, enemies become so victimized or attached to their views that they believe that the other is evil and must be destroyed. The Holocaust and the recent civil wars in Rwanda and Bosnia make this painfully clear. We are all at great risk in these circumstances both as potential victims and as perpetrators. Whenever we demonize, we commit atrocities that in times of peace we would define as deeply wrong. The humiliation and torture of prisoners by U.S. and British soldiers in Iraq's Abu Ghraib prison in 2003 provided a sobering example of this propensity. Yet by studying history and the warrior traditions, including conflict texts like the three-thousand-year-old *The Art of War*, we find that seeking mutual destruction is rarely our best or only available response.

We get stuck in a conflict when we believe it is irresolvable. When we fight with demonized enemies we might then see our only solution as "seek and destroy." Since our world is intimately interconnected, the destruction of our enemies weakens our own position. By removing my opponent, I also lose access to his perspectives, resources, and solutions. We destroy cultures, ecosystems, and species in this way, and ultimately we compromise our own health and safety.

Running away also buys us nothing in the long term. At the beginning of the Bhagavad Gita, an ancient Hindu epic story about life's battles, the kind warrior Arjuna is leading an army into a war against his relatives. He is to fight for what he knows is right. Arjuna starts by begging the god Krishna, who is at his side, not to fight, for he does not want to harm his family and compatriots. Krishna says Arjuna must fight:

> Arjuna said:... Thou holdest that the attitude of detachment is superior to action, then why O Keshava, does thou urge me to dreadful action? . . .
>
> The Lord [Krishna] said:... Never does man enjoy freedom from action by not undertaking action, nor does he attain that freedom by mere renunciation of action.

*When we are faced with an enemy, a person, or group of people that wishes us harm, we can view this as an opportunity to develop patience and tolerance. . . . And the only occasion we have to develop them is when we are challenged by an enemy. So, from this point of view, our enemy is our guru, our teacher. . . a blessing.*

— HIS HOLINESS THE DALAI LAMA

But as Krishna and Mohandas Gandhi, who drew heavily from this text, would counsel, it matters not only that we fight but also how we engage. To find a stabilizing solution, we must stick with the conflict and learn from it. We don't have to like the adversary, and we must justly guard ourselves. However, if we seek to minimize injury while looking for a new answer, enemies can become our allies, and we can work toward a common goal using resources from both sides.

Quantum physicists view the universe as a multitude of interconnected, unique, and necessary parts of a one great living whole. Hindu texts similarly use the analogy that we are all part of one single Self that is everything and lives forever. So I might perceive my opponent as sitting at the end of this Great Being's wild hair, while I am on the tip of its grand fingernail. We all play a unique role and have a valuable perspective. Learning my enemy's perspective can bring me closer to understanding the universe. In the next chapter, we will explore how to identify our enemy so we can safely follow the jackal's example and learn to ask, "Very confusing, I just don't understand. Tell me more. . . ."

CHAPTER TWO

# Identify the Threat

*It is difficult to say who does you the most mischief:*
*enemies with the worst intentions or friends with the best.*

— E. R. BULWER-LYTTON

*Once upon a time, goes a legend among the Nanai tribe in what is now Russia, there lived the Beldy clan, which was always involved in war. They were either attacking or defending and loved to fight so much that they felt lost if they were not in battle.*

*Year after year, more and more men died, and little else was accomplished.*

*Now, one fine day good luck smiled upon the Beldies when some twins, named Chubak and Udoga, were born. Not only was this a good omen, but these boys were indeed special. By the time they could speak, they were so wise that the men and women of the clan often came to them for advice.*

*One day when the twins were young men, a Beldy hunter returned with the news that a weasel had been stolen from his traps by the Zaksuli clan. The Beldy chief yelled, "This is beyond reason and a grand insult! We must go to war."*

*All the Beldy males rushed off eagerly to find their weapons. When the women complained, the men replied, "We are men, and men must fight!"*

*Meanwhile, the women begged the twins, "Udoga and Chubak, tell the men to stay home. No more fighting and killing!"*

*Chubak and Udoga told the women, "We'll see what we can do."*

*Soon the men came to the twins for counsel, and Chubak picked up a warrior's bow and bellowed, "How can this be avenged? If the thief had taken a sable, which has some value, we might forgive him. But a weasel skin? Worthless, they have taken this pelt to shame us. If they don't consider us men, we are good as dead. The Zaksulis have killed us!"*

*Udoga picked up a spear and chimed in, "The Zaksulis have killed us, so all their men must die. Death to the Zaksulis!"*

*"Kill the Zaksulis!" cried the men. "Kill the Zaksulis!"*

*"But wait!" said Udoga. "The Zaksulis are so evil, the place where they live is evil too. We must not let this evil touch us. We must take a vow not to eat any food from their land or drink a single drop of their water."*

*"We take the vow! Kill the Zaksulis!" the men yelled.*

*The women were miserable, but they prepared dried fish, cured meat, and daylily roots to send with their husbands and sons.*

*The next morning, the men loaded themselves up with as much food and water as they could handle. Then, with the twins, they walked toward the Zaksuli village. It was a slow and painful journey with all they had to carry. So the more they walked, the angrier they became at the Zaksulis. Not only did they have to fight, but the Zaksulis made them carry all these heavy supplies!*

*At last they saw some Zaksuli women gathering grain. Chubak called, "Women! Be warned, we are coming to your village to kill all your people!" The women ran off to warn their tribe.*

*"Why tell them we are coming?" said the Beldies. "Those*

*women will get to the village long before we can with all these supplies. The men will hide, and we'll have to wait them out!"*

*"Why worry?" the twins replied. "We are the Beldies."*

*The Beldies reached the village, and the Zaksulis were hiding inside their lodges. They did not want to fight and prayed the Beldies would go home. Knowing that the men would need to hunt eventually, the Beldies hid in the tall grass around the village.*

*The next morning, the Zaksuli men did not come out, but the women waded through the grass to hit the Beldy men with their big sticks. "Go home," they screamed, "go home."*

*"Be brave!" cried Udoga. "Remember, you must never hit a woman!"*

*Chubak called, "We are men. How could a mere woman hurt us?"*

*Each day, they waited for the Zaksuli men, and daily, the women beat them. Then their food ran out. When the men complained, Chubak reminded them, "Remember, we will take no food from this evil place!"*

*Then their water ran out. "Remember," said Udoga. "Not a drop of water from this hell! We've almost won!"*

*And they waited and were beaten a bit longer.*

*"What kind of war is this?" said the chief. "We're so weak that we cannot fight!"*

*"We are men, and what of our honor?" said Chubak.*

*So they waited a bit more.*

*At last an old Zaksuli was sent out with a stick carved with a human face to plead with the Beldy chief.*

*"Talk will never restore our honor," said Udoga. "You must pay a fine."*

*"Yes," said Chubak. "Bring us a great, great gift."*

*The Zaksuli man, worried, asked, "For what are you asking?"*

*Udoga said, "You must gift us, immediately, with a weasel skin and a kerchief to wipe away our shame!"*

*Both sides were amazed and confused. The Zaksuli man hobbled home in joy to retrieve a weasel skin and cloth.*

*The Beldy chief was furious. "What? A weasel skin — that is a great gift? We starved and suffered for a hide and a bit of fabric?"*

*"The weasel skin sent us to war," said Chubak. "Why shouldn't it send us home clean?"*

*When the Beldies returned home, the men told their women about the terrible, terrible war, the worst of all times. They ate and drank for three days straight and vowed never to go to war again.*

When an opponent appears very dangerous, we may want to run away like the Zaksulis, or we may decide to "wage war" like the Beldies. Neither scenario allows us to learn from our opponent. In this chapter, we will explore how to identify our opponents, their distinct characteristics and their inherent risks, so we can respond well and wisely like the twins.

Identifying your opponent is not always easy. We might believe we are battling a child, a needy brother, or perhaps a new state law that is taxing our business into bankruptcy. But, as the twins illustrate in the story above, our true opponents may be hidden. Although the men called the Zaksulis the evil enemies, the Beldies' beliefs about masculinity, honor, and war were in fact their toughest adversaries. To learn from your enemies without bloodshed, or without needlessly destroying another's self-esteem, it helps to recognize against what or whom you are fighting.

For example, I have been known to fight with my children over homework. After a summer of little discipline, each September we all "chafe at the bit," as we'd say in Montana. I nag as they sneak TV when I'm not looking, wait until the last minute to open their books, or stay up too late. Sometimes we laugh through our exchanges; other times there is frustration and tears on all sides.

Who is the opponent in my homework battles? Is it simply the concept of daily assignments? Without them we wouldn't fight, but that's not the whole story. In some cases, I can tell I am battling with my belief that "good mothers make sure their kids do their homework," but I know I am still understanding only part of the story. Sometimes I just hate how little time there seems to be during the academic year. Each conflict brings multiple obstacles, and thus, multiple opponents. To simplify things, we like to lay blame on only one. How about the evil teacher who assigned the math problems? In this example, teachers, time, my beliefs, and the children are all forces to be reckoned with and understood. Homework is an invitation for me to learn about much more than just algebra. I realize that on this battlefield I can improve not only my parenting skills but also my understanding of how to be truly supportive in relationships.

When assessing perceived risks, it helps if we recognize the four key arenas in which we can be threatened. Each of us contains a physical, an emotional, a creative, and an intellectual being, which, when combined, create the unique mysteries that we each are. Around the world, this is how our four aspects are defined:

- Our *physical body* includes our bones, muscles, five senses, and organs. It is also associated with our finances and health, or those things that support our corporeal well-being. Cross-culturally this body is associated with "earth" and is nurtured through good nutrition, exercise, time outdoors, and rest.
- Our *emotional body* contains our feelings, intuition, and personal relationships. Across the globe this arena connects with "water" and as such has no boundaries and is impossible to hold static for long.

We nurture our emotional being through having healthy relationships, accepting our feelings, and sometimes through counseling and silence. The emotional body needs space and gentleness.

- Our *creative body* is equated with the "fire" of our soul, our unique spark and purpose. Creativity is nurtured by the gifts of unstructured time and freedom of expression. The creative body is comprised of vision and unique perceptions. This is the realm of the collective unconscious or spirit.
- Our *intellectual body* is connected to our mind, information, and ideas. It is our personal philosophy of what is right and wrong and includes our self-esteem or ego. Although the ego is given a bad rap, it drives our self-confidence and power to act. Globally, the intellect is associated with "air" and is nurtured through education and games, puzzles, riddles, and so on. This body operates in the invisible world of concepts and philosophy.

When one or more of these areas or "bodies" feels overly vulnerable, we find ourselves threatened or under attack. For example, when reflecting on my homework battles, I find my emotions most under siege. In contrast, the Beldies appear intellectually threatened, since their conflict threatens their fundamental beliefs and their self-worth.

Depending on the type of opponent, some skills will be more helpful than others. The practice of meditation, as defined in chapter 6, can be especially helpful when facing emotionally charged adversaries. When dealing with "horrid" people, like the Zaksulis, we would want to try the techniques described in chapter 8. In the rest of this chapter we will explore the four main opponent types and then apply this knowledge by completing an Enemy Inventory. Throughout the book I have marked each subsection by type to make it easier for you to turn to the most immediately relevant sections:

| OPPONENT TYPE | ICON |
| --- | --- |
| PHYSICAL |  |
| EMOTIONAL |  |
| CREATIVE |  |
| INTELLECTUAL |  |

You will also find a quick reference chart in the appendix that calls out the book's appropriate subsections by opponent type.

##  Physical Opponents

Physical enemies — a thief who breaks into homes around your neighborhood, mice who invade your basement, or a friend who eats the group's provisions on a backpacking trip — threaten our bodily safety. They may be people who you perceive as threatening your environment, say, by polluting the water or by buying up all the land.

Physical opponents initially call for practical short-term ways to protect yourself. Say, for example, thieves break into your car, which is parked on your street. In response you buy a car alarm or move to a safer part of town. A new strain of the flu moves through the country, so you get a flu shot. Seeking to reduce the risk to your physical safety, you may set traps to kill the mice in your garage if you are concerned they may carry the Hanta virus.

We need to remember, however, that there are surely even more thieves, flu strains, and mice lurking about, so ignoring the situation or using destructive means to deal with it leaves everyone compromised in the long term. For example, killing all mice would cause immutable harm to the owl, coyote, fox, and other predator populations. This in turn would affect the ecosystem and human health. Further, these approaches are impractical when dealing with a natural event like a typhoon, since it is impossible to ignore or to get rid of that particular adversary. Instead, to find a lasting resolution with physical opponents, we must move beyond initial problem solving to study our adversaries and look for ways to more successfully coexist.

> *Whoever can see through all fear will always be safe.*
>
> — TAO TE CHING

For example, in my neighborhood, an avalanche is more likely to occur after we have had some warm days in the mountains with additional snowfall. Grizzly bears are more apt to charge right after they have emerged hungry from hibernation. And, with very lax drunk-driving laws in our state, we are justly cautious on the roads after midnight.

Yet complex systems, like people, snow, and bears are impossible to fully quantify. Try to label them or put them in a box, and you will surely be surprised. Those who study chaotic systems have found that in order to understand an opponent, you must instead focus on their individual *rhythms and patterns*. For example, no two hurricanes are alike. Try to exactly measure the landmass touched or water moved, and you will quickly become overwhelmed with data that leads you nowhere. Instead, scientists have learned to back up and see hurricanes as *alive*. Each has a unique personality. If we monitor hurricanes as beings, clear rhythms and distinct patterns will emerge. We can get a feel for their "personality," using this information to determine how to protect those in a hurricane's path.

As we observe one type of system over time, a powerful sense of "knowing our opponent" emerges. Malcolm Gladwell begins *Blink: The Power of Thinking without Thinking* with the story of the J. P. Getty Museum purchasing a small statue supposedly of ancient Greek origin. The seller provided all the appropriate documentation to verify its authenticity. The statue passed rigorous chemical and X-ray tests to prove that it was indeed a rare kouros from the sixth century B.C.E., one of only about two hundred in existence.

Yet, according to the experts, something wasn't quite right. Three art historians then looked at the statue. The first, Federico Zeri, found himself fixated with the statue's fingernails. Evelyn Harrison, one of the world's foremost experts on Greek sculpture, saw the figurine and expressed regret over the Getty's decision to purchase it. She too couldn't say what, but like Zeri, she knew something was amiss. Harrison showed the statue to Thomas Hoving, former director of the Metropolitan Museum of Art. He thought, "I had dug in Sicily, where we found bits and pieces of these things. They just don't come out looking like that." No one could articulate the problem, but instinctive knowing was clearly at work.

Because of these concerns, the museum began to dig deeper and found that the documentation was faulty and that the style of the statue, in very subtle ways, did not match the attested time period. The initial hunches of the three historians showed what hours of research and testing had not. As a result, the Getty Museum updated their catalog to state that the statue might be an authentic kouros or a forgery.

Recent scientific discoveries show that even inanimate objects like rocks are busy with bouncing electrons and neutrons. As systems interact we can learn their patterns of movement and stillness. You might find a rock's personality a bit boring, but just ask a rock climber the attributes and feeling of a favorite outcropping and she'll tell you plenty.

Human opponents also have rhythms and patterns. For example, in conflict, some might trust what they see (physical) over what they feel (emotional). Others might rely on facts and figures (rational) over a hunch (creative) or vice versa. We might attack first and ask questions later. A lawyer friend always asks his prospective clients about their past attorneys to learn what their future relationship might hold. Be it due to nurture or nature, we develop default styles based on our past preferences.

We are mysterious and ever-changing beings, so exercise caution as you try to understand your opponent. If you confidently decide he is an "X," he's sure to shock you by being a "Y." You will best be served by continuing to look for patterns, not by creating strict categories. The more we know about our opponent, the better will be our chances of survival — the basic teaching of a physical enemy. We might ask questions like, What makes my opponent furious? What areas have more crime, and when does it occur? What makes termites attack a foundation? What are the risks for cancer?

> *Observe your enemies for they first find out your faults.*
>
> — ANTISTHENES

For good or ill, interrogators use this method of studying physical opponents as a powerful tactic. Israel's chief interrogator, Michael Koubi, explains, "You have to learn everything about a prisoner and his background. You have to be better than him, wiser than him. If I interrogate a mathematics teacher, I have to know mathematics. If you feel your detainee is wiser than you and you cannot stand head to head, then you must change interrogators."

Bodily opponents can show us our physical limits. How long can we go without eating? How far can we walk? How much can we lift? Personal trainers, great athletic coaches, and Outward Bound instructors can be physical opponents, as can marathons, hiking trips, and exercise classes. Through them we learn how strong and capable we really are.

With physical opponents, we are fighting our own hardwired flight-fight-freeze survival instinct. When we are panicked, our brain stem, or *reptilian brain*, is activated. In this position, we focus on self-preservation and have little interest either in the past or in investigating the future. Notice what happens when you feel physically threatened, say when a local politician passes a law that puts your health or safety at risk. Initially, are you even capable of seeing this person and situation as interesting enough to investigate? Most of us begin with fear and anger. I want to get rid of that awful person, putting her on the first bus to nowhere. When I am focused on survival, threats feel like *things* to overcome instead of people; we turn living beings into objects that can be misused or discarded.

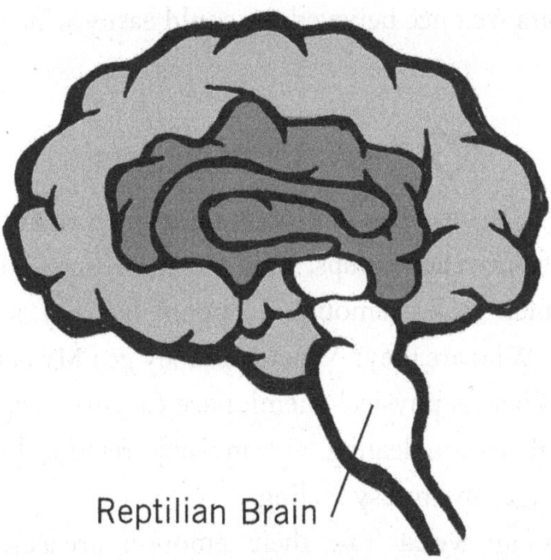

We are taught when we are little what is good and safe behavior and what is not. We might be told, “People who gossip are dangerous” or, “Beware of jealous people.” These intellectual constructs can bring up the fear of a physical threat. In our Russian folktale, the Beldies believed that if their honor was threatened they would die. Was that really true? Unfortunately, the survival-based portions of our brain think so. Meanwhile, stories about what is dangerous and must be destroyed may not be correct and can negatively affect our ultimate survival.

In dealing with physical opponents, we need to assess the inherent contributions and resources that each player brings. For example, symbiotic and often invisible relationships can often provide elegant answers to vexing problems. Coyotes keep the gopher and mice population in check. Rivers flood and bring valuable nutrients to surrounding fields and to the fish population. Bats eat mosquitoes. When we upset the balance without understanding our opponents or this invisible web, we can lose more than we have gained. Also, miscalculating the innate strengths or weaknesses of our opponent can leave us mired in wars we once believed we could easily win.

## ♡ Emotional Opponents

Our feelings can be considered an underground river that feeds the roots of our relationships. Like water, feelings are hard to capture, which makes emotional opponents very interesting adversaries. Who are they? Where did they go? My heart hurts, but why? Whereas physical enemies are easy to recognize and observe, here we are dealing with invisible relationships, emotional sabotage, and messy feelings.

Even though we can’t see them, emotions are a critical part

of our existence. Science tells us that emotions are fundamental in the mammalian experience. Humans and other mammals are equipped with a *limbic system*, which forms the base of our feelings. The limbic, or "old mammalian," brain surrounds the survival-based brain stem and provides our awareness of social interaction, facial expressions, and the feelings of separation and despair.

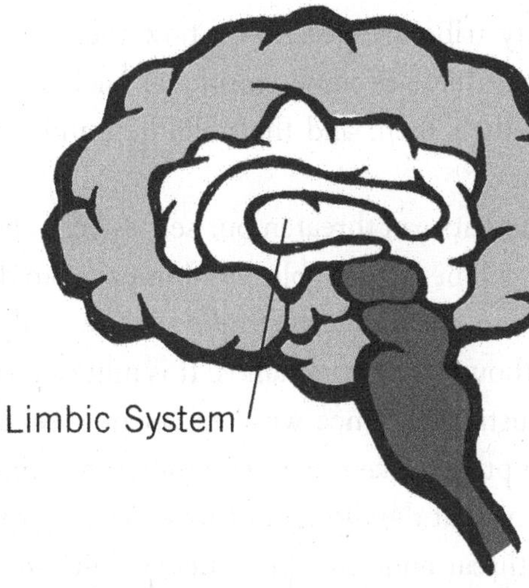


Our emotional health is deeply connected to our physical well-being. Study after study shows that without emotional nurturing, babies will fail to grow, become more prone to illness, or die. Solitary people are three to five times more likely to die early than those with strong, loving relationships. Loss of any relationship places us at risk. As mammals we need connection, love, and friendship, and this makes us vulnerable. "Connectedness assures survival," say psychiatrists Thomas Lewis, Fari Amini, and Richard Lannon in *A General Theory of Love*. When we sense an emotional threat, our limbic system revolts and drives our internal decisions to protect us.

Emotional opponents may be those who threaten our borders, that is, terrorists or foreign governments, or they may even be our loved ones. Our hearts can be broken by anyone, whether we consider them a true foe or a beloved family member. An emotional adversary brings the possibility of loss and thus the painful feeling of grief. These opponents may threaten a beloved object like our home, or they may threaten to dissolve a relationship. When they beg the twins to stop them, the women of the Beldy tribe are describing how their husbands and their love of war have become emotional enemies. They adore their homes, their men, and their children and want to protect them.

Emotional opponents can threaten our self-esteem and create the fear that we will be less lovable and thus easier to desert. Like the reptilian brain, the limbic system cannot be easily controlled by rational thoughts or commands. It is murky territory and can be very frustrating, since we'd rather not feel angry, hurt, or sad. Like a puppy taken from its mother, we may find ourselves howling even at the thought of loss. We may quickly try to remove the threat and attempt to behave differently to keep the relationship in place while carefully watching the result — just as a child will monitor the facial expressions of her mother to figure out what to do next. When the limbic system is under threat, we are in a place of panic.

> *Man is his own worst enemy.*
>
> — CICERO

I often notice how my limbic system takes control when it comes to the safety of my children. As my sons near eighteen, I'll find myself panicking at the thought of them registering for the draft, let alone fighting a war. "I am going to move them both to Mexico," I say while my husband more calmly reminds me that at eighteen our boys will be adults and it will be their decision. Sensing an emotional and physical threat, I'm ready to run to protect my emotional well-being; strong logic isn't the limbic system's territory.

Have you ever had the experience of screaming at a loved one and being completely surprised to find yourself doing so? Or blurting out something you instantly regret? Or procrastinating on an important project, with serious repercussions? The troops are on the move, yet you can't figure out who is leading the charge. They can be found in your inner emotional landscape, but if it is unfamiliar territory for you, it can become difficult to navigate.

Henry had a childhood of neglect. As an adult, whenever anyone — an obnoxious clerk at a grocery store or a family member — started yelling or making noise, he would leave. To him, yelling meant danger. Unfortunately, disappearing made his communication about tough subjects with his children very difficult. To break the fleeing cycle, I suggested that he might want to start by just observing his body response, thoughts, and emotions when someone raises his or her voice.

Developing a deep comfort with emotion is a powerful conflict skill. Sadness, grief, and depression are especially challenging, since we live in a culture that sets attaining happiness as its ultimate goal. When these emotions arise, as they naturally will throughout our lives, understanding and accepting them will increase our ability to lead our internal troops, instead of letting them take us on a wild ride. It takes some degree of fearlessness to recognize our emotions. Looking within can be a pretty terrifying place if we haven't visited it much, so we must begin by having compassion and gentleness for ourselves.

> *Tung-shan was asked, "The normal mind is the way; what is the normal mind?" He replied, "Not picking things up along the road."*
>
> — ZEN PARABLE

Meanwhile, no form on this earth is permanent. All that we

love will ultimately change or die. Our children grow up and may move away. A favorite car wears out. A beloved pet passes away, no matter how carefully we protect it. Although we wish to shield ourselves from pain and to guard what we care about, the world is bent on transforming itself. Therefore, from our emotional opponents we can learn both what is dear to us and what we grasp too tightly, causing ourselves needless suffering.

Facing emotional enemies can be a messy business. We are embarrassed when tears well up in our eyes. Emotions don't always behave as we wish, and the more we try to repress or ignore them, the more they crop up in unexpected places. In essence, they tend to follow the adage "What we resist, persists."

## Creative Opponents

Our creativity is our individuality. It is our unique way of speaking, decorating our home, or dressing. It's hidden in my father's lifelong passion for downhill skiing. It is the spark that has me strolling through art museums every chance I get. Our creative body can be seen as our personality, even as our soul. Creative opponents threaten our distinctive expression. They may teach us how to refine the manner in which we express ourselves, or they might strive to shut us up entirely.

> *As free human beings we can use our unique intelligence to try to understand ourselves and our world. But if we are prevented from using our creative potential, we are deprived of one of the basic characteristics of a human being.*
>
> — HIS HOLINESS THE DALAI LAMA

Creative adversaries can be parents who impose dress restrictions when a teenager opens her closet doors to select an outfit. Our business clients can stifle our creativity, since we must balance their needs with what we long to create. A creative enemy would be anyone who threatens freedom of speech. Outraged art critics became Jackson Pollock's creative adversaries as he developed the genre of throwing paint on his canvases. Creative opponents create doubt and frustration as they press against our deep desire to share our unique vision.

The *neocortex*, the dorsal region of the cerebral cortex that is unique to mammals, handles creative problem solving. This brain, and the prefrontal lobes behind the forehead, engage when we are participating in creative and intellectual activities.

If a creative adversary poses little physical or emotional threat, the neocortex will simply look to inventively resolve the solution. Watch a teenager play with a dress code to uniquely express his style. Or enjoy a lawyer's flair as she deftly interprets the law to find a novel way to win her case. There's no worry about survival here, just a driving need to express.

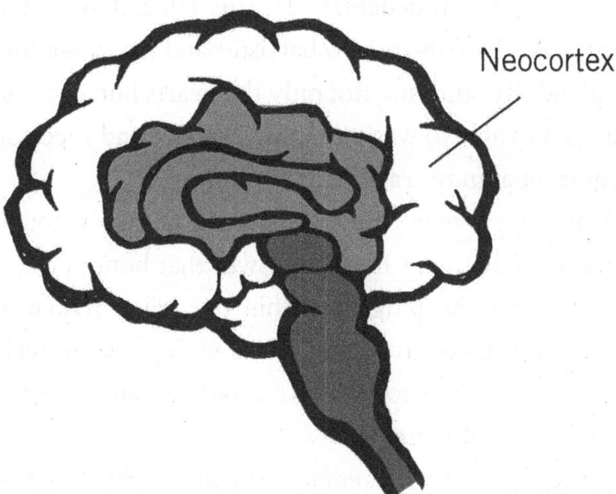


In general, creative enemies constrict our words and actions. Sometimes creative opponents can also physically threaten us when we try to speak the truth. At work there may be an unspoken yet very apparent rule that there are to be no disagreements among employees. So instead of stating our ideas directly in a meeting, we find ourselves carefully choosing words behind closed office doors because we want to hold on to our jobs. We must work to find a way to express what is deeply true *and* to survive. To play well in this creative realm it helps to "know the rules" so you can bend but not break them.

> *Your most unhappy customers are your greatest source of learning.*
>
> — BILL GATES

Mohandas Gandhi, for example, before setting out to win sovereignty for India, traveled throughout the land for a year on third-class trains and by foot to learn about his country and its underlying rules. He asked those he met about their lives and their hopes for India's future. He spoke with Muslims, Jains, Buddhists, Christians, and Hindus. He asked questions of Brahmans and untouchables. To this education he added his expertise as a British-trained barrister and his experience living in England. By studying not only the hearts but also the laws of India, he was able to wage a highly creative and successful nonviolent campaign to transform his nation.

When opponents drive us to act contrary to our morals, internally we battle to find an answer that honors our individual ideals while keeping us within our tribe. It may feel like we are juggling creative approaches with gnawing feelings we can't name. We strive to express our individuality while wracked by fears of abandonment.

Recognize that when engaging with creative opponents we are often planting seeds that may not bear fruit in our lifetimes. Yet we need to keep bringing our ideas forward in creative ways, since we can make a difference, even if it is only for our great-great-grandchildren.

## Intellectual Opponents

Intellectual adversaries threaten truth and reality. They bring into question what is right and wrong, up and down, good and evil. They mess with our plans. Intellectual opponents raise challenging questions: Who is God? Why am I here? What is good? What is bad? We might think we know the answers, we may even have created some good stories to guide us, and then these adversaries come along to befuddle us. Wrestling with intellectual opponents is a practice of looking for a greater truth hiding within sometimes terrible paradoxes.

> *There is no other task but to know your own original face. This is called independence; the spirit is clear and free. If you say there is some particular doctrine or patriarchy, you'll be totally cheated. Just look into your heart; there is a transcendental clarity. Just have no greed and no dependency, and you will immediately attain certainty.*
>
> — YEN-T'OU (828–887)

If my ego is attached to something, say, being a good teacher, wife, or parent, I am constantly trying to understand the rules and be the best. Inevitably, I will misjudge a situation or play poorly by my internally defined guidelines and fall smack on my self-image. And boy, do those bruises hurt!

I call these "sticking points." My sticking points are like big red buttons I wear on my chest that intellectual adversaries love to push. Although you can see them just fine, I hate to admit they even exist. When I teach about this topic, I cut big red circles out of construction paper, which I then affix to my chest with tape. Once, when I was preparing this exercise, I realized that it is simply hidden fear that makes the buttons sticky. We don't want to admit that we worry about money or our professional status, and we pray that no one will notice our vanity or selfishness. We might worry that no one will like us if we are fat, uncouth, or embarrassing.

The stickiness of our buttons is sometimes culturally imposed, and sometimes it comes through our upbringing.

Each culture determines what it believes to be "acceptable behavior." In the United States if I stick out my right hand when I meet you, if you are cultured, you will look me in the eye and also stick out your right hand to shake it. In the many Native American traditions, however, making that kind of eye contact would be considered very bad manners. And in India, if I were to use my left hand to offer you something, you might find me highly impolite or ignorant of that culture's assumption that the left hand should be used only for hygiene.

This is also true in one's home. To be combative and loud at dinnertime might be lauded in one home as preparation for the larger world, while in another that same behavior might be regarded as rude and inappropriate. We are taught in our homes, schools, and communities how to fit in, and stand out, in all the "right" ways. As we are socialized, we form our visions of what is right and good.

Understand that these sticking points are not humorous topics for your opponent. Many people do not wish to be teased about their weight, for example. At an extreme, such as with the issues of when life begins and who goes to heaven, your opponent might even be willing to die for some of his beliefs. Remember that under every button lies fear. Knowing those underlying fears is the beginning of true understanding. Bear in mind that your opponent is trying to hide that fear even from himself, so tread carefully.

Who are intellectual enemies? With intellectual adversaries I am most often fighting my own beliefs. Students who don't like a class I teach might be perceived as intellectual enemies; however, my true adversary is usually the mental constructs I have created around what it means to be good or successful. We all develop our own stories of how the world works. Through them we answer, "Is this a good place to live?" "What constitutes a good person?" and "Who can I trust?" Then, anything or anyone that threatens our viewpoints becomes someone we need to fight. If you were trained as a child to believe that homosexuality is wrong or never to trust people of color, these become the unconscious stories that can create an internal battle cry.

When the beliefs put forward threaten existing structures we are very attached to, we can perceive our enemies as intellectually as well as physically dangerous. All forms of organizations, from churches to businesses, have expelled forward thinkers and truth tellers. During the Renaissance, Galileo's scientific discoveries threatened not only the beliefs but also the underlying power of the Catholic Church. The child who speaks out about familial abuse menaces the safety of the family structure.

With these enemies we have seen the most violence and extreme positions. Heretics and witches were burned at the stake. Bombs are detonated on buses and subways in indealogically opposed cities. Enemies are beheaded, an interesting allusion to the wish to destroy the contrary positions hidden in our minds. The longer a belief system is guarded as sacred and is not subjected to revision, the more dangerous intellectual adversaries become. One woman described her grandmother's fixed beliefs as "a house of cards. By the end of her life, everyone was out to get her."

> *In sparring with a partner, the warrior looks directly into a very accurate mirror — a mirror that kicks and hits back.*
>
> — RICK FIELDS

In contrast, constant engagement with these opponents can help us to expand our understanding of the world. For example, we dream about revitalizing our business or country and entertain wild ideas we can't fully explain but know will work. Inevitably we will find intellectual opponents who say these plans can't be realized. At the beginning of the twentieth century these adversaries said things like "Women don't have the intellect to vote" and "People weren't intended to fly." As a strange by-product of the Enlightenment, when we placed our trust in all things rational, any wild or revolutionary idea became suspect. If we couldn't prove it, we were not to follow it. In *The Answer to How Is Yes*, Peter Block says we have become a culture that responds to vision not with enthusiasm, but with doubts about implementation.

Yet, as we are sent out to find facts, instead of being diverted from our vision we can be strengthened. For example, when I first discovered *The Way of Conflict* philosophy, it lived more in the realm of inner knowing than in data. But through writing and teaching, I was pushed by tough opponents who inspired more research and, thankfully, improved my presentation and understanding.

When we can open ourselves to the idea that what we thought was wrong might also be right and what we believe was good could also be bad, we learn. It is in those moments of paradox that truth emerges. Opposites merge, and we learn that beauty can be found in horror, that love has little to do with perfection, and that we can all be equally confounded by life's mystery. With the help of our intellectual adversaries, our wild plans can soon become reality.

## Using the Enemy Inventory

In the appendix you will find a quick reference chart calling out the sections of this book especially relevant to your opponent's type. I have developed a brief assessment to easily uncover this type. With the "Enemy Inventory," you will think of a conflict, name your potential opponents, and list everything you feel is threatened. Then you will answer a set of questions in table format to assess the overall type of threat this conflict brings. The assessment then reveals a dominant opponent type so you can focus on the skills relevant to that type contained in the remainder of the book. Before you fill out your own inventory, let's first look at the following two examples as illustrations.

### *Example 1: The Sister-in-Law*

In this example, let's use the crazy-making sister-in-law, Suzie Politics, from the introduction, who pushes her political beliefs every chance she gets.

#### *An Enemy Inventory*

1. Think of a conflict. Who are your opponents? They could be people, beliefs, or anything that is threatening you. List them below and star the major players:

    - My sister-in-law *
    - Her beliefs
    - Her political party *
    - My unwillingness to confront her

2. What is threatened? To what categories do these belong (physical, emotional, creative, or intellectual)? List them below:

    - My relationship with my brother (emotional)
    - My beliefs (intellectual)

- Our country's well-being if her party succeeds (physical)
- My composure and self-esteem (emotional and intellectual)
- How I act around my family (intellectual and emotional)
- My peace of mind (intellectual)

The numbers in the sample enemy inventory on the next page represent the responses for Suzie as the adversary. To use the enemy inventory, you rank your responses to the five questions listed from 4 to 1, with 4 being your most likely response. Then total your responses vertically. The highest score determines the type of threat posed by the opponent. Refer back to the sections of this chapter describing physical, emotional, creative, and intellectual opponents. You may fill out this table multiple times to assess different adversaries within one conflict.

| ENEMY INVENTORY | | | |
|---|---|---|---|
| DOES YOUR OPPONENT THREATEN YOUR: | | | |
| Physical safety? 3 | Self-esteem or emotional health? 2 | Freedom of expression? 1 | Beliefs, reputation, and worldview? 4 |
| IF SUCCESSFUL, COULD YOUR OPPONENT CAUSE: | | | |
| Financial or physical hardship? 4 | Loss, grief, or sadness? 1 | Time or creative constraints? 2 | A sense of unfairness or confusion? 3 |
| IS YOUR FIRST REACTION IN THIS CONFLICT: | | | |
| To create additional security controls and protection? 3 | To shut down to protect against emotions such as despair or loneliness? 2 | To become overwhelmed? 1 | To start thinking about the situation and the opponent — you can't let go? 4 |
| WOULD YOU CALL YOUR OPPONENT: | | | |
| A competitor for resources? 1 | A threat to your relationships with self and others? 3 | A threat to your rights and freedom? 2 | Painful, ridiculous, crazy, or misguided? 4 |
| WITH THIS OPPONENT, DO YOU NEED TO BE MORE LIKE A(N): | | | |
| Warrior? 3 | Monk? 1 | Activist? 2 | Psychologist or lawyer? 4 |
| TOTALS: | | | |
| Physical 14 | Emotional 9 | Creative 8 | Intellectual 19 |

Suzie is first an intellectual and then a physical opponent. She threatens my beliefs, ego, and, I believe, my country. I can feel frozen or powerless when she appears in my living room, and I am unwilling to confront her behavior. I spend hours on the phone telling my friends what a pain in the neck she is.

Crazy makers like Suzie, or the Zaksulis from the story above, can blind us to our true reality and become our worst enemies. We are taken hostage by the other's behavior. Why do we not ask her to stop? Why not state our beliefs or ask tough questions? If we hate a trait, like forcefulness or closed-mindedness in another, we will most certainly hate it in ourselves. We miss its potential strengths and uses. When we are dealing with abhorred traits we can turn a primarily intellectual conflict into a physical battle of survival, and at an extreme wage war against this evil other, as with the Beldies.

With these enemies, as we will explore in more detail in chapter 8, most often I need first to confront a hidden internal opponent. The good news is that with these opponents, often there is no need for direct confrontation. If the Beldies could have recognized that this was a crazy-making conflict, and not an issue with the Zaksulis, there would have been no need for battle.

Since Suzie also poses a potential physical threat, I need to do my research on the potential risks of this opponent. In this case, it would probably be by more clearly understanding the proposed policies and power of her political party. Physical enemies demand that we pay attention and understand their underlying resources and personality so we can better protect ourselves.

If action is warranted after I make peace within, I can act from a calmer and more creative place. I might talk directly to my sister-in-law and explain how I dislike political discussions at family gatherings. Perhaps I will make my own beliefs clearer and try to better understand hers, setting ground rules for subsequent exchanges. If I can come to terms with a crazy-making behavior within myself, I regain personal power and room to move. The battle can be won without wanton destruction or suffering.

### *Example 2: Homework*

Below illustrates the characteristics of an emotional and creative threat using my earlier homework example.

#### *An Enemy Inventory*

1. Who are your opponents in this current conflict? They could be people, beliefs, or anything that is threatening you. List them below and star your major opponents:

    - The concept of homework *
    - Cultural values *
    - School *
    - Time or my beliefs about time
    - My children
    - My beliefs about relationships
    - My definition of the role of mother *

*(Notice that here I am working primarily with beliefs and concepts.)*

2. What is threatened? To what categories do these belong (physical, emotional, creative, or intellectual)? List them below:

- My future relationship with my children and husband (emotional)
- My self-esteem (emotional and intellectual)
- My children's future (emotional)
- My children's self-esteem (emotional)
- The teachers calling me in to say I'm a poor parent (intellectual and emotional)
- My personal time (creative)
- Time we could use to play together, if only they would get the darned homework done (creative and intellectual)

The numbers in the sample enemy inventory on the next page represent the responses for homework as the adversary. As in the previous example, to use the enemy inventory, you rank your responses to the five questions listed from 4 to 1, with 4 being your most likely response. Then total your responses vertically. The highest score determines the type of threat posed by the opponent. Refer back to the sections of this chapter describing physical, emotional, creative, and intellectual opponents. You may fill out this table multiple times to assess different adversaries within one conflict.

## ENEMY INVENTORY

| DOES YOUR OPPONENT THREATEN YOUR: | | | |
|---|---|---|---|
| Physical safety? 1 | Self-esteem or emotional health? 4 | Freedom of expression? 3 | Beliefs, reputation, and worldview? 2 |
| **IF SUCCESSFUL, COULD YOUR OPPONENT CAUSE:** | | | |
| Financial or physical hardship? 1 | Loss, grief, or sadness? 2 | Time or creative constraints? 3 | A sense of unfairness or confusion? 4 |
| **IS YOUR FIRST REACTION IN THIS CONFLICT:** | | | |
| To create additional security controls and protection? 1 | To shut down to protect against emotions such as despair or loneliness? 2 | To become overwhelmed? 4 | To start thinking about the situation and the opponent — you can't let go? 3 |
| **WOULD YOU CALL YOUR OPPONENT:** | | | |
| A competitor for resources? 2 | A threat to your relationships with self and others? 4 | A threat to your rights and freedom? 3 | Painful, ridiculous, crazy, or misguided? 1 |
| **WITH THIS OPPONENT, DO YOU NEED TO BE MORE LIKE A(N):** | | | |
| Warrior? 1 | Monk? 4 | Activist? 2 | Psychologist or lawyer? 3 |
| **TOTALS:** | | | |
| Physical 6 | Emotional 16 | Creative 15 | Intellectual 13 |

This is primarily an emotional and creative conflict. I am working with intangible relationships, cultural values, and institutions. With emotional opponents, I work to know myself better and to look gently within. I struggle with fears of loss and emotional pain. These opponents teach the capability to let things be as they are.

I am also battling the educational system and its belief that kids need to do homework. When I am pushing against an organization or institution, it is usually a sign that I have met a creative adversary. Time as a component of the battle is another indicator that I am facing a creative opponent in this conflict. Therefore, I need to learn the rules or laws of the institution to creatively respond and resolve my issue.

We can each perceive different threats from a common opponent. For example, in the homework conflict, I am not overly concerned about the risk to my physical safety. However, women often draw a direct correlation between their physical safety and the health of their relationships. We are especially vulnerable to feeling physically threatened if we are dependent on our spouses or children for money. In contrast, men may address a relationship threat as purely emotional or as not a problem at all. Traditionally, women more often ask, "Who will care for me when I grow old?" and thus are more vigilant about their relationships.

Now it's time for you to do your own inventory. In a journal or on your computer, answer the following questions.

*An Enemy Inventory*

1. Think of a conflict. Who are your opponents? They could be people, beliefs, or anything that is threatening you. List them and star the major players:

2. What is threatened? To what categories do these belong (physical, emotional, creative, or intellectual)? List them.

Answer the five questions on the next page by ranking your responses across from 1 to 4, with 4 being your most likely response. Then total your responses vertically. The highest score determines the type of threat posed by the opponent. Refer back to the sections of this chapter describing physical, emotional, creative, and intellectual opponents.

| ENEMY INVENTORY | | | |
|---|---|---|---|
| **DOES YOUR OPPONENT THREATEN YOUR:** | | | |
| Physical safety? ___ | Self-esteem or emotional health? ___ | Freedom of expression? ___ | Beliefs, reputation, and worldview? ___ |
| **IF SUCCESSFUL, COULD YOUR OPPONENT CAUSE:** | | | |
| Financial or physical hardship? ___ | Loss, grief, or sadness? ___ | Time or creative constraints? ___ | A sense of unfairness or confusion? ___ |
| **IS YOUR FIRST REACTION IN THIS CONFLICT:** | | | |
| To create additional security controls and protection? ___ | To shut down to protect against emotions such as despair or loneliness? ___ | To become overwhelmed? ___ | To start thinking about the situation and the opponent — you can't let go? ___ |
| **WOULD YOU CALL YOUR OPPONENT:** | | | |
| A competitor for resources? ___ | A threat to your relationships with self and others? ___ | A threat to your rights and freedom? ___ | Painful, ridiculous, crazy, or misguided? ___ |
| **WITH THIS OPPONENT, DO YOU NEED TO BE MORE LIKE A(N):** | | | |
| Warrior? ___ | Monk? ___ | Activist? ___ | Psychologist or lawyer? ___ |
| **TOTALS:** | | | |
| Physical ___ | Emotional ___ | Creative ___ | Intellectual ___ |

## Key

A. *Physical*: something that might cause you physical discomfort, pain, or loss. Attacks your finances, shelter, food sources, or physical protection.

B. *Emotional*: something that could cause emotional pain. Might hurt your feelings, cause you sadness or grief, or injure a relationship you value.

C. *Creative*: something that might take away your free will or freedom of expression. Constricts your ability to be uniquely you.

D. *Intellectual*: something that threatens your worldview and beliefs. Attacks your understanding of what is good/bad and right/wrong. May affect your identity and self-understanding.

It's easy to become distracted in conflict. Like the Beldies, we can find ourselves fighting the wrong opponents, which can be quite painful. We don't always have time to complete the inventory before responding to a threat, and we might need to just dive in to fend off an attack. To get a high-level assessment of the opponent and the type of threat you face, instead ask yourself, "What is the worst thing that could happen?"

If the worst thing that could happen involves bodily harm, like dealing with a grave illness or fighting terrorism, I am facing a physical opponent. In contrast, in my homework example, I worry most about my children's future and our relationships: love thus connects us to emotional opponents. Third, if I am blocked from being able to express myself, like painting in a new style like Jackson Pollock did, I am facing a creative opponent. If the worst thing that could happen is having our personal identity or beliefs threatened, like the Beldies, we are facing an intellectual opponent.

Now that we have identified the enemies around us, in the next chapter we will look at the opponents within. A traditional Sufi tale tells of an ailing king who sent for a physician-sage to heal him. The sage did not want to go, but the king's soldiers grabbed him and brought him to the castle. The king demanded that the physician heal him from a strange paralysis and, if he did not, the ruler would have him killed. The physician said, "I need complete privacy to treat you." So the king sent everyone away. The physician then drew a knife from his bag and said, "Now I will seek my revenge on you for threatening my life" and ran at the king. The king, forgetting his affliction, jumped up and ran around the room trying to escape the apparently crazed doctor.

> *Good people are good because they've come to wisdom through failure. We get very little wisdom from success, you know.*
>
> — WILLIAM SAROYAN

The sage escaped from the castle closely pursued by the guards, while the king remained unaware that he had been cured from his paralysis by the only effective method available.

We too may need extreme methods to free us of a strange paralysis. Whether or not our external enemies know or care that they are teaching us is not the point. Their presence can become our healing balm, regardless of their underlying intention. As we will see in the next chapter, we all can easily become frozen like the king by internal adversaries. By recognizing the natural barriers that being human brings we can manage and even overcome without duress.

CHAPTER THREE

# Meet Your Inner Opponents

*Don't cling to your own understanding. Even if you do understand something, you should ask yourself if there might be something you have not fully resolved, or if there may be some higher meaning yet.*

— DOGEN

*This is a story of another tiger from long ago. It comes from Tibet.*

*When the world was young and animals spoke, an old tiger named Tsuden went out hunting. As he crept along the banks of a stream a frog saw him and was afraid. He thought, "This tiger is coming to eat me."*

*When the tiger came near, the frog hopped out in the open and yelled, "Hello, where are you going?"*

*The tiger answered, "I am going into the woods to hunt something to eat. I haven't eaten for days, and I am weak and hungry. You're awfully small, but perhaps I will eat you."*

*Squaring his shoulders and swelling up as big as he could, the frog replied, "You should know that I am the king of frogs. I can jump any distance and do anything. For example, see this river? Let's see who can jump across."*

*"All right," said the tiger.*

*As the tiger crouched to jump, the frog slipped in close and took the end of his tail in his mouth. When the tiger jumped, the frog was thrown up the bank across the river and over the tiger. After jumping, Tsuden turned and looked into the river for the frog. But as the tiger turned, the frog said, "What are you looking down there for?"*

*The tiger whirled around, very much surprised to see the frog way up on the bank behind him.*

*Said the frog, "Now that I beat you in that test, let's try another. Suppose we both vomit."*

*The hungry tiger had nothing to show for this effort, but the frog quickly spit up some tiger hair.*

*The tiger, astonished, asked, "How did you do that?"*

*The frog replied, "Oh, yesterday I killed a tiger and ate him, and these are the last few hairs that aren't quite digested."*

*The tiger thought, "What a ferocious creature. Yesterday he killed a tiger, and now he has jumped farther than I did over the river. I must get away before he eats me." He slunk away and then began to run as fast as he could, up the mountain.*

*He met a fox coming down, who asked, "Why are you running so fast?"*

*"I met the king of all the frogs, a formidable beast. Why, he eats tigers and can jump across the great river without a care."*

*The fox laughed and said, "You are running away from a little frog? I am only a little fox, but I could put my foot on him and kill him."*

*The tiger answered, "I know what this frog can do, but if you think you can kill him, I'll go back with you. I am afraid you will get frightened and run away, so we must tie our tails together."*

*So they tied their tails fast in many knots and went to see the frog, who was looking as important as he could by the river. He called out to the fox, "You're a great fox. You haven't paid your toll to the king today. Is that a dog you've got tied to your tail, and are you bringing me my dinner?"*

*Guessing the fox had tricked him into returning to the frog king to be eaten, Tsuden took off at a run, dragging the fox behind him.*

*If they are not both dead, Tsuden still runs today.*

When faced with immediate physical danger, we instinctively react in order to survive. When terrified, as the tiger was facing his amphibious foe, we move into a fight (have the fox kill the frog), freeze (become immobilized at the side of the river), or flee (run away!) reaction. However, as we can see from the story above, the fight-freeze-flight instinct can also be a tough internal enemy, since the terrified tiger misses his true position with the frog. In a fear-filled state, we do not learn from our opponents, nor are we able to take advantage of all our resources.

Recently I awoke to a radio report on Cambodia and about how the Pohl Pot regime's murder of millions does not appear in that country's history books. Then, eating breakfast, I read the newspaper. "Dear Abby" that day provided "Fifteen Warning Signs of a Batterer," and there was a short piece on an Oregon father who had killed his wife and three kids in the woods, stabbing the eight-year-old daughter eighteen times.

Like the tiger, I could feel my "flight" reaction kick in; I wanted to crawl back into bed and hide. The intentional malice was so potent in these stories. My understanding simply could not grasp them. Among the morning's dirty dishes, I asked myself, in the face of genocide, parents murdering children, and domestic abuse — three of the more abhorrent acts of humankind — how do I dare talk about learning from our enemies? How in the world can I write that destructive enemies deserve *anything*, let alone our respect? I wondered if my beliefs were just ridiculous naïveté. "Run, run," said my brain. "Give up the crazy pursuit of studying conflict; it's too dangerous!" I was filled with fear and self-doubt and felt paralyzed.

Soon after two dear, wise friends added some perspective. My neighbor Pat asked, "Is not death our ultimate enemy? And without death, there is no life. Without pain, there is no joy." Later my friend Marcus told me how when a close friend was dying of cancer, another horrible opponent, she said she wouldn't have traded the experience for anything: "If you had asked her what five things she was grateful for in regard to the cancer, she could have written a book."

My friends woke me out of a fear-based reaction that had stopped me in my tracks. To return to learning, I need to accept my current position and open myself to this enemy-teacher paradox. Domestic abuse, murder, and terminal illness are very real, whether we face them daily or not. These types of "teachers" don't fit the "sweet grandmother who teaches second grade" model. A tiger is still a tiger. When we wrestle with tough opponents, we may not survive. So we need to fight smart not only to improve but to better protect ourselves. My hiding from terrible enemies will not make them go away. In this chapter we will explore the different ways we limit and further expose ourselves to danger, including our natural brain reactions, our fear of loss, our innate love of stability, and our unwillingness to face those we believe to be bad. With awareness of our limitations we can overcome them to more successfully engage with our opponents. First we will look at how our own brains can trip us up.

## Our Wonderful, Wacky Brains

The architecture of our brain influences how we perceive, respond to, and remember a situation. As discussed previously, it consists of four main regions: the reptilian brain, the limbic system, the neocortex, and the prefrontal lobes. Each can influence our actions, depending on both internal and external conditions. How much we perceive, remember, or maneuver in conflict will depend on which region is running the cerebral show.

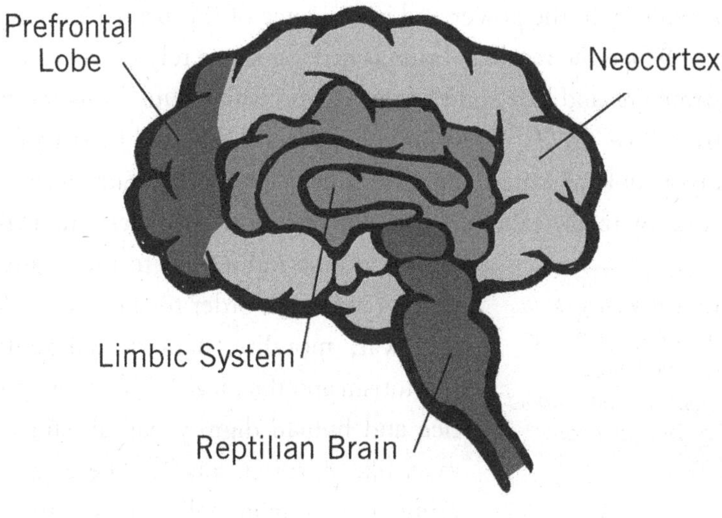


When we are startled, some of the signals received through our senses are short-circuited to the amygdala, a small almond-shaped structure in the central limbic system. Brain researcher Dr. John Ratey calls the amygdala an "investigator into the ambiguous" that decides if fight, flight, or freeze is warranted and, if so, activates the reptilian brain. The reptilian or motor brain focuses on immediate survival. Its reaction, says Ratey, "is rough and crude but fast." Our heart rate and blood pressure increase, our breathing quickens, and the motor system pumps up the adrenaline, preparing us in a life-or-death situation to run faster than we ever have before.

However, when in fight-flight mode, we are not focused on the long-term effects of our actions, nor will we remember if these reactions worked in the past. For example, when a person is starving and needs to feed her family immediately, cutting down all the trees around her home makes sense. Simply put, wood = cash = food = existence. Later, when this resource is depleted, she might wonder why she made this terrible mistake. Yet despite the drastic nature of the solution, she has survived, testimony to the power and importance of this primal strategy.

When the reptilian brain is driving us we rely on very basic strategies and lose sight of our relationships. Our focus moves from "we" to "I." "This moment I am at risk, and I must solve my problem" might be the internal response. Survivors of Auschwitz, for example, describe how both the jailers and prisoners became indifferent to the misfortune of others in order to stay alive: "In this war, morality, national solidarity, patriotism and the ideals of freedom, justice and human dignity had all slid off man like a rotten rag. . . . There is no crime that a man will not commit in order to save himself," wrote one survivor, Tadeusz Borowski. Writer Primo Levi, another survivor adds, "It was a Hobbesian life, a continuous war of everyone against everyone." To save ourselves, we are able to dehumanize our opponents and destroy without guilt.

> *Whatever a rival may do to a foe, or a vengeful person to the one he hates, a wrongly applied mind would do more damage to him than that.*
>
> *Nothing that a mother, father, or other relative might do would do more good for him than a mind well controlled.*
>
> — DHAMMAPADA, 3

In contrast, when our relationships are threatened, the limbic system, in the center of our brain, works to take hold. Also survival focused, the limbic system works in the past and present to keep those we love safe. As a parent, this is our "mother bear" instinct. Come near my children, and I will bite your head off. For some in Auschwitz, the relationship portions of their brains controlled their actions, as with parents who stole so that their children might eat. One Buchenwald survivor writes, "Father and son...hungry together, offering their bread to each other with loving eyes."

> *Better a patient man than a warrior, a man who controls his temper than one who takes a city.*
>
> — PROVERBS 16:32

Our children need boundaries, and our nurturing nature ensures that we keep an eye on our charges. My friends and I laugh as we admit how much our love — the limbic system — dictates that we lock our teenagers in monasteries until they turn twenty-one. Yet this "to your room, young man" approach is not beneficial to them or to the development of their ultimate independence.

Complex problem solving, learning, and self-control occur primarily in the neocortex, along with the prefrontal lobes, which regulate emotions and support decision making within a social context. Although we are wired to go first to the motor brain and limbic system, we can, like the crafty frog, overcome this urge and re-engage these upper realms of the brain. It appears that when we perceive a threat, received information actually takes two brain routes for processing. The short route (the "low road") to the motor system, as discussed above, ignites our immediate fight-flight mechanism. The second, slower route (the "high road") heads to the neocortex and the prefrontal lobes to give a more accurate assessment, a more considered response. Capturing the information that the slower cortex path provides takes skill and practice.

Throughout history, spiritual and martial arts traditions have developed principles and techniques for staying relaxed

> *O Lord, remember not only the men and women of good will, but also those of ill will. But do not remember all the suffering they have inflicted on us; remember the fruits we have bought, thanks to this suffering — our comradeship, our loyalty, our humility, our courage, our generosity, the greatness of heart which has grown out of all this, and when they come to judgment let all the fruits which we have borne be their forgiveness.*
>
> — UNKNOWN PRISONER IN THE RAVENSBRUCK CONCENTRATION CAMP

and keeping the neocortex involved when in conflict, so that we remain open to new information when responding to an opponent. One effective technique for retaining our creative capacities in battle is to regard our opponents as worthy and even sacred. In part 2 of this book, we will discuss how by holding this perspective we can protect not only our physical bodies but also our basic mental health.

Another brain barrier is found within our existing neural pathways. Say I was taught as a child that tall men were not to be trusted. A connection would be created within my mind that links the input and reaction "There's a tall man" and "Be afraid." As I grow, if this neural pathway is used again and again successfully without question, it will become stronger, an ingrained highway of sorts. Or, if I was raised in an arid climate, when I see rain, I may have an ingrained neural pathway that instantly registers "good" or "relief."

Neural pathways make it very challenging for us to open ourselves to new information. To test the strength of these internal roadways, scientists asked participants to name card after card placed in front of them from a seemingly normal playing card deck. However, some of the card's colors had been switched, that is, the four of hearts was now a black card, and the three of spades was red. Participants would correctly name card after card until reaching the switched-color cards, calling the four of hearts, a four of spades. It took the participants going multiple times through the deck, consistently misnaming the switched cards, before they began even to *sense* that something wasn't right.

These mental models also influence our basic memories. Study after study shows that people have an amazing tendency to remember things that didn't happen. Since the 1970s Elizabeth Loftus has been pioneering the study of false memories. In two recent studies, Loftus found that one quarter of adults, when queried about childhood events, will "remember" experiences that never occurred.

> *If a man should conquer in battle a thousand and a thousand more, and another should conquer himself, his would be the greater victory, because the greatest of victories is the victory over oneself.*
>
> — BUDDHA

Meanwhile, existing emotional networks will create memory selectivity so that we may also not remember what actually did occur. Lewis, Amini, and Lannon wrote, "If an emotion is sufficiently powerful, it can quash opposing networks so completely that their content becomes inaccessible — blotting out discordant sections of the past. Within the confines of that person's virtuality, those events didn't exist. To an outside observer, he seems oblivious to the whole of his own history." For example, severely depressed people will blot out any memories of happy times in their childhood, denying them vehemently when confronted by well-meaning siblings or parents.

Our memories are also malleable. Our brains recategorize memories continually, depending on our current environment and mental health. I might initially remember a meeting with a boss favorably as he discussed my future career possibilities. If, during the following weeks, he fires a number of other employees, I might begin to remember the meeting as "bad" and filled with innuendos that he plans to let me go.

There are also limits to what we can perceive. Although information surrounds us, because of the nature of our equipment we often miss sounds, images, and smells. Notice how much more data even the family dog can pick up with his eyes, ears, and nose than we can. If this isn't humbling enough, we are programmed only to notice and process information that makes sense to us.

For example, I spoke with a man in his thirties who worked in an office adjacent to the World Trade Center on September 11, 2001. He recounted how that fateful morning he was standing by a window, printing out a stock report when he saw tons of paper falling from the sky. He thought, "I wonder why we are having a ticker tape parade today?" When a friend mentioned that something had happened to the Twin Towers, he went out on the street and watched the smoldering buildings in its plaza with curiosity. "I couldn't get it; the whole situation just didn't make sense. I look back on how I behaved and where I stood and shudder. It was as though I suddenly woke up standing outside. A friend and I then took off as quickly as we could. That park was completely covered in rubble minutes later."

It is daunting to realize how much we must overcome within our own physiology to learn or notice something new. Warrior instruction in the different traditions is not so much a training of the body as it is one of the mind. In part 2, we will focus on sharpening our mental capabilities so that we might better gather, record, and use the information that surrounds us.

## ♡ The Fear of Loss

Another way in which we limit ourselves is by fearing loss. The truth is, *every resolved dispute includes loss*. In other words, for a conflict to end, some sort of death must be involved. I will need to let my initial position die so that a larger solution can emerge. I might have to give up previously held beliefs. Every time we are taught something new, our old understanding of the world must be left behind.

We naturally fight against death in any form, be it physical, intellectual, emotional, or spiritual. We learn early to see death as our ultimate enemy. Yet intermediate deaths and rebirths are fundamental elements of our existence, a truth reflected in our myths and shown to us by nature's seasons; things perish and create space for the new to emerge.

Our own physical death is the most obvious example, but we experience many physical minideaths throughout our lives. We let go of our previous forms of childhood, adolescence, child-bearing adulthood, as we become elderly. Even though some of these "deaths," like leaving an adolescent body to move into motherhood, might be welcome transitions, the death of our youth might still sting. If we are lucky to live long enough, these small deaths will occur regardless of whether or not we embrace them. Fighting illness, we may leave one physical state to be reborn into another. For example, those who have survived cancer often find not only their physical bodies but also their emotions and beliefs completely transformed.

> *Knowing others is*
> *intelligence;*
> *knowing yourself is true*
> *wisdom.*
> *Mastering others is a*
> *strength;*
> *mastering yourself is*
> *true power.*
>
> *If you realize that you*
> *have enough,*
> *you are truly rich.*
> *If you stay in the center*
> *and embrace death*
> *with your whole heart,*
> *you will endure forever.*
>
> — LAO-TZU

Fearing the loss of a relationship can stop us from having crucial conversations with friends and family. The thought of a friendship dying thwarts our courage. We are afraid that if we confront the problems, the connection might end. You may know some static couples who ignore the fact that they do not communicate honestly out of fear of being alone in their old age. Ironically, it is just these conversations that are needed to keep the relationships strong and thriving.

Whenever we reassess our ideas and beliefs, we will experience creative and intellectual deaths. Think of your initial reaction when someone tells you you are wrong or that you are seeing a situation incorrectly. Many of us tend to close down, since we need our stories to hold our understanding of the world together. If you take away my understanding of reality, how will I survive? Yet those who are strongest and most mentally vital in their elder years consistently test and let die their beliefs, making way for new thoughts and innovation.

Be gentle with yourself. Since we each fight death as our ultimate enemy, it is inherently difficult to confront life's risks and trials. Yet, remember, without death, there is no life. Its presence makes this time brief and creates its preciousness. As consultant and teacher Patrick O'Neill advises wisely, "Befriend death. Make it instead your ally."

## Our Love of Stability

We are also constantly fighting a universal battle of needing conflict and innovation while wanting peace. Over 13 billion years ago, in the beginning microseconds of the universe, a great disequilibrium occurred. Although it's hard now to envision, before this disequilibrium everything was the same. Afterward, we had *difference*, or the ability for up and down to exist, and for peacocks, elephants, and you to be created. With difference we always have diverse things that bump against each other, making conflict a fundamental component of our expanding universe. On some levels, we like change and conflict. It shakes things up, creates new opportunities. Yet, at the same time, like all systems in the universe, we yearn for peace and stability, or what scientists call *homeostasis*.

Our wish for homeostasis keeps us from bringing up a tough topic with our spouse or floating a radical new idea with our boss. If things seem quiet, let's just let sleeping dogs lie. We'll take a cease-fire, even if we know it might not lead to lasting peace. Conflict is dangerous. After World War I the situation in Germany was dire, and fascism soon began its ascent. Ignoring the troubling circumstances did not make them disappear, and some might say that a craving for stability lead to the resulting bloodshed of 1939–1945. Yet, who would want to rock the boat after experiencing so much pain and loss in earlier years?

> *Boldness has genius, power, and magic in it.*
>
> — JOHANN WOLFGANG VON GOETHE

We struggle with hopelessness when facing large and powerful institutions like governments, schools, and corporations that do not wish to change. "How can I make a difference?" we may exclaim, seeing a fight against the giant both as dangerous and as a waste of time. We want these institutions to change and evolve, but we also fear stirring things up. This universal battle between a desire for evolution and creativity and a desire for stability will always be with us. Neither is good or bad. Neither alone creates happiness or true balance. We need both. This innate conflict in our lives can best be understood through the Taoist yin/yang symbol (illustrated on next page).

Within the need to shake things up lies a desire for stability, just as the white circle resides within the black. And within our

need to let things be lies our innate longing to learn and grow, just as the black dot resides within the white. Taoism teaches us to balance the opposites, whatever they may be. If we are bent on change, we are counseled to also embrace stability. If we want to let sleeping dogs lie, it might also be time to shake things up. "Stable change" or "changing stability" are our best long-term bets for thriving.

## Our Unwillingness to Face Extremes

We also limit ourselves with our own basic beliefs. In them we hide our most fundamental stories about who is good and bad. Dark and "wrong" characteristics in others repel us. We might walk into a room and then want to turn around and run like the panicked tiger when we see a boastful oaf bragging in the corner, a slick-talking politician ranting, or an insecure shrew backstabbing another. We may think, "If these are my opponents, why would I want to learn from them, let alone be in the same room with them?" Yet, each of those people might hold valuable solutions to our most perplexing problems.

When we were young, we were a handful, to be sure. We were naughty and nice, boastful and humble, manipulative and innocent. Our families and culture took charge and told us which traits might best help us fit into our communities. And our stories about what it means to be a good girl or boy took hold. Meanwhile, we were still naughty, nice, boastful, humble, manipulative, and innocent, but after our enculturation we acknowledged and developed some of these traits, while others we relegated to an internal closet.

Crazy people scare us. As social animals we expect others to behave in a certain socially acceptable manner. If someone does something culturally associated with aggressive behavior, he or she will create confusion. If I say hello to you as we pass on the street, I will expect some kind of acknowledgment; that's what nice and what safe people do. But if you glare at me or stop and stare, my internal alarms will go off. You are not doing what I expected, so what might you do next? I might then envision the worst scenario and think I must stay away from you or, at an extreme, get rid of you before you destroy me. When we are disoriented, we are more apt to return to a survival-based reaction.

> *It's a human being you're dealing with, not a devil, and you can feel a human connection with him, and realize at the same time that it's important to separate the person from the problem.*
>
> — BILL URY

However, you may have glared at me because you are hard of hearing and have misinterpreted my greeting. Or you may suffer from autism and may not understand my verbal and facial cues. You may be from another culture where greetings on a street might warrant stopping and speaking with that person in depth. How can I stay open to gathering information before jumping to conclusions? When we are able to move beyond our confusion and fear, transformative experiences will follow.

In 1971 C. P. Ellis and Ann Atwater became friends and

community allies. This tidbit became national news since at that time, Ellis was the Exalted Cyclops of the Durham, North Carolina, Ku Klux Klan, and Atwater was a strident African-American civil rights activist. In a way, the two had much in common. Both had come from lower-income districts in Durham and struggled to make ends meet. Ellis's rise to power in the KKK mirrored Atwater's climb in the ranks of community activists. Ellis and Atwater recognized that engaging in city politics might benefit their respective causes, so they found themselves serving on the same committee dealing with the desegregation of their local schools.

However, before they became friends, both saw the other as the ultimate enemy. Atwater recalls when she was growing up, the local KKK killed an African-American mail carrier after allegations that he had had a relationship with a Caucasian customer. Ellis spent his childhood learning that "niggers" were the source of the family's financial stress and community ills. In the initial steering committee meetings, Ellis exploded, "If we didn't have niggers in the schools, we wouldn't *have* any problems. The problem here today is *niggers!*" Ann shot back, "The problem is that we have stupid crackers like C. P. Ellis in Durham!"

Ellis and Atwater were asked to cochair a ten-day city council conference to openly address the schools issue. Very reluctantly they agreed. Ellis said, "We were asked to meet to plan this conference over lunch. I had never sat down to eat with a black person. The closest I had ever been to one was on the street."

As they planned the conference over the coming weeks they had to talk to and learn from each other. They realized that they were both serving on the education committee because their children were having similar serious problems at school. When they tried to set a location for the conference, they found a surprising mutual terror of the other's neighborhood. And they discovered other similarities stemming from the terrible low-income struggles of their community.

By the end of the ten days, Ellis had resigned as a Klansman and forged a deep friendship with Atwater that continued for at least twenty-five years. At the conference's close, he announced to those present, "I used to think that Ann Atwater was the meanest black woman I'd ever seen in my life." He then explained how talking to her had changed his view: "She is trying to help her people, just like I'm trying to help my people."

> *I keep my ideals, because in spite of everything I still believe that people are really good at heart.*
>
> — ANNE FRANK

In some cases, we might deem extreme people or actions as evil. *Evil* — even the word can make us nervous. So, how do we learn from those who have moved outside the realm of human decency or even humanness, such as murderers, rapists, the criminally insane? Radical extremists and their evil acts make us want to turn away. We hope they will disappear. We don't want to learn from them, let alone acknowledge their presence. We cringe as we read about torture, abuse, and genocide, knowing it's impossible to say that malevolence doesn't exist. People can do very destructive things and use their creativity in ways that make our skin crawl.

When something or someone is branded as evil, learning seems out of the question. "Learning from the Devil" — isn't that the ultimate taboo? Would I not be aligning myself with the truly malevolent and thus become possessed? Yet three beliefs about evil cause me to recognize that even wicked enemies have something to teach. A fear-based aversion to wickedness that keeps me running and off balance is rarely the superior position of a warrior.

First, I believe that there is relativity in any action. As Rumi said, "What is a highway to one is disaster to the other." The nature of evil is comparative, whether we like it or not.

Let's use genocide and the polio vaccine as examples. Think of the misery and terrible legacies genocide causes. Now think about how the polio vaccine saves millions and millions of lives. Would we not label human genocide as evil and the polio vaccine as good?

Now pretend you are a rhinoceros. Once your kind roamed Africa. There were plentiful food sources and territory. But now your species' existence is endangered by the advance of humans into your home. If I were to ask you, "When you think of genocide and the polio vaccine, which is good and which is evil?" what would you answer? As a pachyderm, you would probably believe that controlling the human population would be a good and holy thing. You might add, "Let's remember that humans are killing themselves, after all. Is that not simply a natural, evolutionary approach to population control?"

Meanwhile, if I asked you about the polio vaccine, which has been a major supporter of the twentieth-century surge of the planet's human population, you might say, "Jonas Salk is evil. Through his actions, millions of my kind have died. Such evil acts from one little human."

Second, I believe that the Christian story of Satan as the great enemy has interesting implications for how we view evil. Elaine Pagels, in *The Origin of Satan*, reveals that the Devil as a personified evildoer is a relatively new phenomenon. In the Old Testament, Satan was not a distinct entity but a term given to angels sent by God to save us from harm or to obstruct us so that we could learn something. The Hebrew term *satan* simply describes an adversarial and not necessarily malevolent being. Pagels states, "As literary scholar Neil Forsyth says of the *satan*, 'If the path is bad, an obstruction is good.' Thus the *satan* may simply have been sent by the Lord to protect a person from worse harm." In the Book of Job, for example, the *satan* is a supernatural messenger from God's royal court. It wasn't until the Gospel of Mark in the New Testament that Satan appeared as a separate ruler of an evil realm that should be destroyed at all costs. Mark appears to be the first sacred text in the Judeo-Christian tradition that completely removes parts of the universe from God.

This New Testament view of separateness is not a cross-cultural principle. True, we now find aberrations of this conviction in radical Christian, Jewish, and Islamic thought, yet in Tibetan Buddhism demons "have no objective reality but are viewed as misunderstood energies within the human mind." In the Hindu tradition, demons are given instructions and promises from gods. From the Taoist viewpoint, all that exists is a critical and valued part of the greater whole and is necessary for the stability of the universe.

Perceiving one's own group as superior and devaluing another, however, is a universal practice. In ancient Egypt, the word for "Egyptian" was *human*. The Greek word for "non-Greeks" is *barbarian*, mimicking the gibberish of those who did not speak the language. Human beings like to identify with a group or tribe and use labels and values to differentiate themselves from others.

> *Darkness cannot drive out darkness; only light can do that. Hate cannot drive out hate; only love can do that.*
>
> — MARTIN LUTHER KING JR.

Pagels adds that "the use of Satan to represent one's enemies lends to conflict a specific kind of moral and religious interpretation in which 'we' are God's people and 'they' are God's enemies, and ours as well." Thus we create a history that can justify "hatred, even mass slaughter." If another is possessed by the Devil, the story goes that he or she is not human or of God and therefore loses basic rights and respect. The manifestation of this belief appeared in the Salem witch trials, the Spanish Inquisition and, sadly, in modern-day conflicts including the murdering of homosexuals and the bombing of abortion clinics.

Pagels believes that this satanic enemy was initially created to demonize the Jew, who did not see Jesus as the Messiah. The Romans, who probably crucified Jesus on charges of seditious behavior as a radical Jewish activist, were then placated through these writings. The Evil One then became not the Roman Empire, but the unconverted Jewish community. According to Pagels, this enemy making supported the wider acceptance of Christianity and also created centuries of Jewish persecution.

> *What is hateful to yourself, do not do to your fellow man. That is the whole of the Torah, and the remainder is but commentary.*
>
> — TALMUD

Recognizing that it is our culture that labels things as evil has allowed me to step back a bit and, if nothing else, look at who has done the classifying and why. In the Rocky Mountain region, wolves have borne the opposing labels of "evil" and "savior of the ecosystem" within the last one hundred years. In our nation's history, women with the same training have been called both "satanic witches" and "midwives." The satanic label is a powerful tool to quiet dissent and stop our evolution.

A third reflection on the concept of evil is that we tend to demonize large groups, when in reality only a small percentage could be deemed wicked. For example, C. P. Ellis found his stereotypes shattered as he began to interact with the Durham black community, where as before a white woman touching the hand of a black man made him almost ill. Returning to the lessons of Auschwitz, author Tzvetan Todorov, in *Facing the*

*Extreme*, notes, "Camp survivors seem to agree on the following point: only a small minority of guards, on the order of five to ten percent, could legitimately be called sadists (and thus abnormal)... Himmler supposedly even gave instructions to remove from duty any SS man who appeared to take pleasure in hurting others." As Primo Levi states, "Monsters exist, but they are too few in number to be truly dangerous. More dangerous are the common men [who mindlessly or fearfully followed orders]." For Levi, who wrote books about the Holocaust for forty years after his internment, it was critical to distinguish between the group and the individuals who belonged to it, thus creating a clear contrast between himself and the Nazi regime. He never formally forgave his captors, nor did he exclude them from the "circle of humanity."

We should understand against whom we are fighting. For example, Ellis and Atwater found their ultimate opponents to be not one another, but the unjust social structure of their community. The word *evil* is sometimes used as an enemy that makes us clutch in fear and closes off our ability to respond creatively. What happens within when you hear a country's leader call another government an "evil empire"? When another deems a group as satanic, should we not question this assumption before following their edicts?

Our internal challenges add to our struggles. We must contend not only with our external adversaries but also with our brain, our fears, our love of stability, and our beliefs and the cultural stories that surround us. We never have a full and accurate picture. All these ways in which we limit and trip ourselves up are also important short-term survival tools, yet we must recognize and contend with them, since none supports us over the long term.

Knowing that enemies surround and are within us can feel pretty grim. Yet each opponent brings amazing potential benefits. Before we move on to techniques for facing our opponents, as we will do in the second half of the book, in the next chapter we will learn what wonderful surprises can be in store for us whenever we choose to meet our adversaries. We will now explore four major gifts our enemies can bring and how everyday folk have gathered these rewards to improve themselves and the world.

CHAPTER FOUR

# Reap the Rewards

*One very important ingredient of success is a good, wide-awake, persistent, tireless enemy.*

— FRANK B. SHUTTS

*In China, a well-known thief was conscripted into the military. A huge battle was about to be waged with a much larger army. The night before the thief's army was to advance, the thief asked to see the general, saying he could end the war before it even began. "You are crazy. The general will never see you," said a captain. But because of the wise look in the thief's eyes and his insistence, the captain took this message to the general.*

*The general had heard of this famous thief and thus asked that the conscript join him in his grand tent. The thief bowed and told the general, "If you will give me three days, I can win this war," and then shared his idea. Because the general was wise in the Taoist ways, he said he would assure the thief three days without battle to carry out the plan.*

*Later that night the thief snuck through the enemy camp and into the opposing general's tent and stole the general's sword. He took the sword to his commander, and the next morning the wise general presented the weapon to the opposing army with great fanfare.*

*That night, the thief again snuck into the opposing general's tent and, this time, stole the general's bedspread. This prized possession was returned to the opposing army with a formal, public ritual the following morning.*

*The third night, the thief returned to the opposing general's tent and took his decorated helmet.*

*At dawn, there flew the flag of surrender over the opposing general's tent, signaling the end of the war. "What are you doing?" exclaimed the opposing general's advisors. "We have their army outnumbered ten to one; why would we surrender?"*

*"Because," replied the general, "tonight they would have taken my head."*

Why should we try to learn from our opponents? This path requires discipline, commitment, and practice. It takes work. In the short term it is not the easiest path — our ingrained quick reactions are. So when looking for an appropriate analogy to explain why striving to stay close to our opponents to improve is worth the effort, I think about swimming.

I have never been a great swimmer. Even though I took lessons as a child, my strokes are inefficient and I tire easily. I feel that I am constantly fighting against the water and can't wait to finish. In any type of open water I get pretty nervous. I don't much like the sport and look for excuses not to participate. And I have missed out on a number of fun adventures as a result.

My friends who swam competitively tell a different story. They find swimming meditative and beneficial to their bodies, minds, and spirits. They happily spend hours completing laps in the pool or out playing in a lake or ocean. Although they respect water's dangers, their practice and study of this element provide them with confidence and the ability to enjoy it.

The general wise in Taoist ways demonstrates the benefits of warrior technique and ample practice at conflict. He is calm and keenly aware; enemies, war, and thieves do not unnerve him. The general demonstrates creativity and comfort in great adversity. He appears willing to use all the resources available to him, including felons, to bring peace and stability. He extends respect to all around him; as master warrior, he understands that the most skillful strategy is to subdue the other's military without battle. Although he appears ready to fight, the general sees no need to go to war, just as swimmers know you don't need to attack the water to get to the other end of the pool.

> *Everyone has a spirit that can be refined, a body that can be trained in some manner, a suitable path to follow. You are here for no other purpose than to realize your inner divinity and manifest your innate enlightenment. Foster peace in your own life and apply the Art to all that you encounter.*
>
> — MORIHEI UESHIBA, FOUNDER OF AIKIDO

We too can become better through confrontation without direct battle. This chapter provides examples of allowing our enemies to lead us to new answers and considering them as neither bad nor good, but as potential teachers. Sure, there are skills we can apply, like using a good stroke in swimming to support us, and with practice conflict can become easier. Yet regardless, we each can have everyday hero experiences if we're willing to try. As I researched this book, I asked two questions of clients, acquaintances, friends, and family, many of whose answers are included within this chapter:

- Who or what has been your most formidable opponent?
- What have you learned as a result?

I would explain that an opponent can be a person, an illness, or anything that has caused problems. Some answered that they had no opponents, so I would ask instead:

- What is one of the greatest challenges that you have overcome?

As they answered, I witnessed great courage, creativity, and radiance. When confronted, challenges bring out our essential beauty. As novelist José Saramago says, "It is in moments of extreme duress that the spirit gives the true measure of its greatness." But the person often had to first experience great hardship or misery before she received conflict's gifts. Once earned, these benefits fell into four distinct categories, each of which we will explore below:

- Clarity
- Connection
- Strength
- Inner peace

These rewards match the benefits promised by the dedicated warrior training of an ancient mythical kingdom, Shambhala, a utopia where all lived deeply happy and peaceful lives. The sacred Tibetan texts prescribe a set of Shambhala warrior teachings with which anyone today can create harmony and joy at home, within a community, or beyond. This path draws heavily from Buddhism, as do all the Eastern martial arts. It also holds the warrior practices of the indigenous Bon culture, Taoist philosophy, and Japanese samurai. The Shambhala warrior has keen awareness. She is compassionate and fearless. With an indestructible core she is both strong and deeply at peace. We will return to the Shambhala tradition to illustrate each benefit.

In asking the two questions, I also realized that some types of opponents (physical, emotional, and so on) are more challenging than others, depending on our acquired skills and past experience. For example, one friend who has practiced martial arts most of his life has no difficulty facing physical opponents, such as someone throwing a punch or a health or financial issue. Yet he is not comfortable with emotional combatants. He is honest with me only because he knows I won't fall apart: "I hate when people cry. I don't know what to do when that happens." In contrast, others had more practice with creative adversaries and deftly worked through the problems that they presented. It comes down to technique and practice; our tougher opponents appear in areas with which we are most unfamiliar.

> *Life is so generous a giver, but we, judging its gifts by their covering, cast them away as ugly or heavy, or hard. . . . Everything we call a trial, a sorrow or a duty, believe me, that angel's hand is there; the gift is there, and the wonder of an overshadowing presence.*
>
> — FRA GIOVANNI

Sometimes the interviewees had overcome a tough challenge and could call it "the best worst thing that had happened to me." However, some were still thick in the battle, and I watched them bravely fighting to discover the hidden insight. The importance of certain opponents can remain a mystery throughout our lives. One woman's father had an affair and eventually married his mistress. Sixty years later she could not see any value in this experience: "All I know is that divorce is extremely painful for children. My mother died not knowing why this had happened. It was just terrible."

During the interviewing process, I became fascinated by our culture's "fighting" professions. We hire lawyers and doctors to battle using law or medicine. Activists are devoted to clashing with adversaries against perceived injustices. Also, we ask corporate executives to lead organizational armies to fight against competitors. Wondering if these might be considered our culture's modern-day warriors, I interviewed a representative from management, oncology, activism, and law to discover their wisdom from the battlefront. Although news reports abound about executives, lawyers, and doctors who have not acted with honor and discipline, I believe the individuals described below demonstrate what we can each gain by actively fighting a good fight and staying close to our enemies.

We will now examine the rewards of clarity, connection, strength, and inner peace and how others have received these from some fearsome opponents.

## Clarity

*A Profile in Learning: From a Warrior Executive*

*My most formidable opponent? That's easy: John Doore. In the early 1980s I had just taken a Human Resources director position in a large manufacturing company. I should note that I was the first female manager in another division of this company ten years earlier. I was pushing against the glass ceiling with every promotion.*

*Soon after I took the new job, a woman manager came to me and said, "You probably won't do anything about this, but there is a vice president here who has been sexually abusing different young women in this division for about twenty years. Everyone knows about it, but nothing has ever been done." It was reported that this executive was engaging in the worst kind of sexual harassment: making inappropriate comments to young women employees in his department, touching them, even fondling them. These young women — frequently relocated from rural areas and having little sophistication about the corporate world — did not know what they should not tolerate and when they could say no and still keep their jobs.*

*Well, I knew I needed to do something. However, the company had never been through a sexual harassment investigation before, and legislation had only recently been passed that outlawed sexual harassment and abuse in the workplace.*

*I went to my immediate manager and explained the situation. He sent me to one of the top executives, who was Doore. Doore urged me not to bring the investigation since it would damage the career of a senior level executive who had made significant contributions to the company. "He's a good employee," he told me. "Don't do it."*

*But I realized at that point I would lay my job on the line to push for an investigation. It got worse before it got better. Doore spread the rumor that I was pursuing the investigation because I was "a man-hating, premenopausal b_____." That really hurt, yet it was a bit funny, as I spent each evening trying to sort all this out with my husband of twenty-five years. I had taken on what we used to call "the old boy network," and they knew how to protect their own. (It turned out that there had been a series of reported incidents over the years that had not been dealt with.) I was going to be the whistle-blower against a powerful system.*

*Then my boss suggested that a man should do the investigation because as a woman my objectivity would be questioned. I had to explain that this was part of my job description, and if I couldn't do it, I would need to resign. I threw my badge on the table. I knew my chances for advancement were gone, but I didn't care.*

*My boss relented and let me lead the investigation. I learned how to find political allies. The corporate lawyer and I teamed up, knowing that the new legislation required both of us to investigate and confirm the claims. We came to a settlement whereby the offending executive left the company. My career was over with that company, and it was one of my proudest accomplishments. Through my experience of dealing with this opponent, I became much clearer about what I stood for and my life mission.*

Our opponents can wake us up to who we are and for what we are willing to fight. Like the corporate executive above, there comes an event, a turning point where our essential purposes blaze forth. If we are both strong and vulnerable enough to weather this event, our new lives take form. Azim Khamisa's twenty-year-old son, Tariq, was jumping into his car in San Diego to deliver pizzas when he was murdered by a fourteen-year-old gang member, Tony Hicks. Khamisa was a successful investment banker who had emigrated from Kenya as a young man, and his life was ripped to pieces. "In our [Muslim] ritual, the father stands in the grave to receive the child's body into his arms. I did not want to leave him there alone. I wanted to go with him." As Khamisa worked through the grief and rage, his calling became crystal clear: "I would help my country protect all its children. I would become the foe, not of my son's killer, but of the forces that put a young boy on a dark street holding a handgun."

After creating the Tariq Khamisa Foundation (TKF), Khamisa found his thoughts returning to the killer's family. Eventually he contacted Ples Felix, Tony Hicks' grandfather and guardian, who Khamisa describes as a kind, smart, caring man who holds a master's degree in urban development and is a project manager for the city of San Diego. "He dearly loved his grandson and was devastated by what the child had done — on the first night that he had ever defied his grandfather and left the house to meet with the gang." Now Felix and Khamisa work together through TKF to end child violence. In eight years the foundation has reached over 350,000 elementary- through middle-school children. "Our goal is to create leaders who are peacemakers."

Life-threatening opponents can bring priorities and our path into clear focus. Irene, seventy, who has fought chronic bronchitis for most of her life, explains, "This disease has almost killed me a few times, so I am doubtful I have a long life expectancy. I hate the illness and fight it, but through it I realized how to live in the present. I try to observe, take in all around me, and live for today. Meanwhile, I have seen friends who die soon after they retire and never experience the wonder of life. Bronchitis thankfully didn't give me that option." As expert surfer and doctor Mark Renneker remarks, "One of the things I love about my work as a physician, and I work with cancer patients and people with life-threatening illnesses, is to see... literal transformation... they begin to live, truly live almost for the first time... those life-changing events can come from illness. They can come from revelation and they can actually come from, for me anyway, big wave surfing."

> *It's not whether you get knocked down, it's whether you get back up.*
>
> — VINCE LOMBARDI

Our adversaries might uncover our hidden potential and unrealized dreams. Peter, a man I deeply admire, struggled daily with school. He tells stories from the 1930s when he spent most of fourth grade punished in the coat closet. He couldn't read until he was eleven and thus was held back an academic year. He continued to battle his way through the educational system until he dropped out of school at seventeen and lied about his age to get into the navy.

While on a ship during World War II, he noticed how much better the college-schooled officers' quarters were than those of the enlisted ranks. One day Peter was ordered to carry an eighty- to one hundred-pound Freon container from the first to the fifth deck. At five-foot-five, weighing only about 140 pounds himself, he struggled up the steps as the ship rolled back and forth. Using the most direct route, he snuck through the officers' area to reach the fourth deck. A mean-spirited officer named Lukey met him there and sent him back down to the first deck with orders to come up through a more circuitous route on the ship. "Just because he was an officer, he could do that to me. He made up my mind. I was going back to school and would never treat someone as he had treated me." So at the end of the war Peter enrolled in the Maritime Academy and graduated first in his class. He then fought in the Korean War as an officer and today is a very successful entrepreneur.

"When I was a child, my father told me nightly the importance of education. It wasn't until I met Lukey and lived on that ship that I believed him. That set direction in my life and made me a lifelong learner," Peter adds.

Gerald Jampolsky, in *Good-bye to Guilt*, proposes that there are only two emotions, love and fear. Although this depiction of our vast emotional landscape might seem overly simplistic, the internal conflict between fear and love does seem to lie at the base of all our contests. Love makes us brave and willing to confront life's challenges. It can be love of self, nature, or family that makes pain and hardship bearable. "Everybody loves something," Chögyam Trungpa Rinpoche, who brought Shambhala to the West, once said, "even if it's only tortillas." Fear exposes what we love. Love pushes us to face fear and define what matters.

The underlying clarity brought forth by recognizing our love can then become a sword that allows us to cut through our apathy and fear. Eve Ensler, women's rights advocate and performer of the *The Vagina Monologues* and *The Good Body*, talks about this powerful weapon: "I've seen awful things — refugee camps, burned women, and skulls on riverbanks — but I have a clarity of purpose [to end violence toward women]..., which allows me to see all that and keep going." Yet we must be careful, since the power that strong intention yields can be used for healing or destruction; just look at the Crusades or Al Qaeda as worrisome examples of strong but misguided purpose.

> *What keeps us alive, what allows us to endure? I think that it is the hope of loving or being loved.*
>
> — MEISTER ECKHART

Adversity brings transparency to our sometimes uncounted blessings. Jan Chestnutt had lived her entire life in Vero Beach, Florida, but three consecutive devastating hurricanes in 2004 crystallized for Jan the community's core beauty. Throughout the storms, neighbors stepped in: "In our area, we became each other's keepers. If someone evacuated, we had their house keys. We put up shutters on everyone's homes and had a daily check-in. It was clear then what was most important. Our neighborhood made communal pots of hurricane soup with ingredients from our melting freezers. We cooked it over camp stoves with gas siphoned from our cars." When Jan visited a local radio station, the only available information source for many days, the disc jockeys invited her into a studio with no roof overhead. The announcers stayed on the air twenty-four hours a day, huddling close to a generator-run air conditioner propped up on a chair. Amid the ruined citrus groves and beach hotels, Jan exclaimed, "I'm in the right place and so lucky to live here."

## Connection

### A Profile in Learning: From a Warrior Doctor

*I fight against death.*

*As an oncologist, I have the difficult duty of sharing dire prognoses with patients and their families. I can get caught in the cross fire of their anger and grief — something we were not trained to deal with when I was in medical school. That wish to shoot the messenger is alive and well in the exam room, unfortunately. My work is to stay calm and present for others as they come to terms with the battle ahead.*

*One of my most formidable opponents has been a young cancer survivor whom I have treated off and on over the past several years. She may not live very long because of what she has suffered. Yet she does not take advantage of the time she has. I want her to see that she has beautiful children and a great life that could be enjoyed right now. It is a tough situation, and I have cried with her. Although I get frustrated at times, she has taught me patience, tolerance, and compassion. Do any of us truly appreciate what we have?*

*As doctors, we are trained not to get too close to our patients so that we can hold on to our objectivity. Regardless, over the years I have met many wonderful people and end up seeing them quite often during their treatments and follow-ups. You can't help but form a relationship. I still become emotional when I think of one of my first patients in practice. She was a lovely woman, just ten years older than I, who was gentle and maternal. She survived a bout with breast cancer and was healthy for the next ten years. During that time, her son died of testicular cancer. Her cancer returned in a very aggressive form and took her a year or so after. She was a beautiful soul — it is still a loss.*

*During my oncology fellowship I worked for a much-credentialed department head. We had two patients who partially responded to experimental treatment, kind of a last-ditch effort to save them. Eventually, however, they both began to die. The department head was very involved and optimistic until the patients were deemed incurable. Then he refused to see them. I have never forgotten that; it was then that the patients needed us by their side, even though it was a losing battle.*

Since many physicians deeply care about their patients and want to alleviate their suffering, their work comes from their heart. It's a paradoxical situation: How to be tough and tender at the same time. Empathy creates vulnerability in us all. And the resulting emotional pain can be as horrible as physical ailments, if not worse, since we ache from invisible wounds.

Ultimately our heartbreaks can not only support our personal well-being, they can also benefit and connect us to the greater community. The staff of Landmine Survivors Network always pairs recent landmine victims with survivors who have already moved through the incredible grief and are now thriving. These everyday warriors light the path for the recovering victims and transcend any feeling of separateness.

Duncan Grady's story illustrates this heart-opening process of leadership. Grady was raised on the Siksika/Sac Blackfeet reservation in Montana until age twelve, when he was removed to a residential school and then raised by an adoptive family. Of Native American and Scottish descent, Grady returned to his childhood home as an army veteran thirteen years later. "When I came back from Vietnam, I had a lot of wounds, emotional, spiritual, and physical. I thought maybe by returning to the reservation that I might be able to heal." A Blackfeet elder, Chester

Battering Shells, took him aside upon his arrival and said, "I can tell you were a good soldier; now we will teach you how to be a warrior." And his nine-year warrior training with Siksika/Sac, Blackfeet, and Oglala peoples began.

We must decide during each confrontation under what flag we wish to fight: the flag of our family, our company, or our country. Does it carry solely a picture of me? Depending on the battle, the flag will be different, yet selecting a banner that reflects a connection forged by our broken hearts can transform our lives. Now a psychotherapist and university professor, Grady carries a new flag into daily battle. He remarked on his journey: "As soldiers we were taught to fill our backpacks to survive. As a warrior I was taught instead to carry as little as possible and to follow a path of service. My injuries that had become barriers instead are now bridges. We all can connect through our wounds, since through our pain we can experience how others might be suffering, and we are drawn to help. There I am connected to myself, my community, and all my relations."

> *You cannot prevent the birds of sorrow from flying over your head, but you can prevent them from building nests in your hair.*
>
> — CHINESE PROVERB

Compassion is the ability to feel the pain, and the joy, we share with others. "Common passion" is another way to describe it. True compassion is founded in the understanding of our interconnectedness, or as Grady explained, in knowing our place with all our relations. Through our pain, we connect with another person's sadness and understand her experience. We can also relate to and celebrate her accomplishments. Our hearts crack open, and we recognize our commonality.

Through this bond, we can find comfort in the knowledge that we are never truly alone. Nuala O'Faolain, author of the bestselling autobiography *Are You Somebody?*, describes the first rule of making one's memoirs compelling as "begin with a broken heart." Self-described as an unremarkable middle-aged woman, she shows how magnetizing honestly relating her pain can be. After the end of a fourteen-year-long relationship, she says, "I was as dreary as you can be and still function.... Thousands of people who are not of my culture, gender, or class — who don't even share my first language — wrote to me about my first book.... We all share the human condition."

Through loss, we learn tenderness, compassion, and tolerance. Chögyam Trungpa Rinpoche writes on Shambhala training, "For the warrior, this experience of a sad and tender heart is what gives birth to fearlessness. Real fearlessness is the product of tenderness. It comes from letting the world tickle your heart, your raw and beautiful heart. You are willing to open up, without resistance or shyness, and face the world. You are willing to share your heart with others." Through the cracks in your heart your spirit reaches out and connects with others.

> *When the mind sees this, it will rid itself of attachment which holds that "I" am beautiful, "I" am good, "I" am evil, "I" am suffering, "I" have, "I" this or "I" that. You will experience a state of unity, for you'll have seen that all of [hu]mankind is basically the same. There is no "I." There are only elements.*
>
> — AJAHN CHAH, "BODHINYANA"

Our opponents often appear to deepen our understanding of the mysterious nature of relationship. Karen adopted a girl and a boy from India. Her daughter is a bright light who at six practices ballet and is learning to read. Her son, aged four, who was adopted at a year and a half, suffers from reactive attachment disorder. "After the adoption, he became progressively more violent," Karen explained. "He cannot be held or touched by women."

After the child went through years of attachment therapy, Karen's ex-husband finally took sole custody of their son and lives out of state.

Karen explains:

> "I love my son but realize that being with me was terrible for him. I have changed my thoughts in every way about love, nature, nurture, and babies. My son was injured in his connections, and I have learned there is no rhyme or reason, since my daughter went though more horror than he did, but his anger goes deep. Even through it broke my heart, to best serve him, I needed to let him go.

> *I was born when all*
> *I once feared —*
> *I could love.*
> — RABIA

> "I once believed love could cure anything, but this is simply not true. Love, I have learned, comes in many different forms and has no concrete definition. As a mother I know no greater love than that with my daughter. As a mother with my son, I know no greater pain than letting go. As a partner I know love as the continuous circle of what all came to life through your words and markers."

## Strength

*A Profile in Learning: From a Warrior Activist*

*When George W. Bush came into office and began undoing key environmental policies, I thought I wouldn't be able to sink much lower. My entire career as a scientist has centered on protecting grizzly bears and other predators. With a government focused on delisting these animals as endangered species, I knew we were in for a real fight. Bush is clearly just a symbol, I know, but he's an opponent. In general, there is great misunderstanding about the importance of valuing our country's predators.*

*On a day-to-day basis, I battle government agencies that are responsible for implementing these new policies. There have been times where they have misinterpreted data or it has appeared that they have even hidden critical information. Their leadership is extremely politically adept and controls all the funding for critical recovery programs. These issues make me want to pull my hair out. In these low times, I have been losing hope in our environmental community. I just don't see the young people stepping forward effectively. I had been doing this for twenty-five years and was getting very tired of fighting.*

> *On the path of service, we are constantly given feedback, which helps along the journey of awakening.*
>
> — RAM DASS AND PAUL GORMAN

*About a year ago, I didn't think I was going to be able to keep going. Between the lack of government support and of new blood in the movement, I just wanted to give up. After some extremely vicious battles between some local government leaders and me, I hit my personal bottom. On a whim, I went to a yoga retreat with my husband to try to recover. I found that I could use yoga and meditation to pull myself out of my depths.*

*In addition, I have taken to writing poetry and painting, and have written two plays about the life of the grizzly bear. Art, story, and spiritual practices buoyed me in ways I could never have imagined. I am now considering creating workshops with other activists to teach them how to hold on to their hope and spirit.*

*Without my adversaries, I don't think I would have known about these tools. I have learned that no matter how low I go, I have the ability to get myself out. That is very empowering and energizing. I feel like my core is strengthened, and I can keep on fighting. If we have to sue the government not to de-list the grizzly, so be it.*

Opponents can uncover profound inner resources. As we can see in the above account, plunging into our lowest depths can bring us back stronger and more resilient: "The ideal of warriorship is that the warrior should be sad and tender, and because of that, the warrior can be very brave as well. Without that heartfelt sadness, bravery is brittle, like a china cup. If you drop it, it will break or chip. But the bravery of a warrior is like a lacquer cup. . . . If the cup drops, it will bounce rather than break. It is soft and hard at the same time," writes Trungpa Rinpoche.

Through our trials we begin to accrete layer after layer of learning and conditioning. Repetition is the foundation of yoga, athletics, and the martial arts. Try. Fall down. Try again. Fail so terribly that your heart and ego crumble. Now try again. One friend battled throughout her childhood with the constant negative feedback of an alcoholic father. With her mother's love as her base, she grew year after year in resolve. Like a lacquer cup, she now appears unbreakable. When she decides to do something, we stand out of the way and watch, knowing that in whatever task she undertakes she will succeed. She is a fighter whom you always want at your side.

Michal (pronounced "ME-hall") and her family abandoned their farm on the Gaza Strip in 2000. Among the Israelis who left Gaza that year, Michal, at seventeen, shielded her baby sister with her body while their bus, filled with women and children, was pelted with rocks. "My parents were born in Gaza, so we left all that our family had known. I have lived in war and terror most of my life. At eight, I was called upon to comfort my best friend after her father was murdered by Palestinian extremists. We wondered each morning leaving for school and work if we would see each other that evening." Nonetheless, when I met Michal, I encountered a warm and vibrant spirit who was in the midst of a yearlong trek that included backcountry camping in Chile, Cuba, and Mexico. When I asked her who had

> *Everyone needs a warm personal enemy or two to keep him free from rust in the movable parts of his mind.*
>
> — GENE FOWLER

been her worst opponent, she simply replied, "It is fear. I know it is necessary, but I have missed so much when I let my fearful self overwhelm me. I am now learning how to work with it so I can see the world and work with troubled youth. I assess the risks and know that my heart will be broken along the way."

Facing those who wish us ill can teach us how to stand strongly for what we believe is right. "I find my worst opponents have been those who truly wanted to harm me on the mat," says Tom, a master aikido instructor. "This is the opposite of the aikido philosophy, so their anger has caught me off guard and they have hurt me. I have had to learn to meet an attacker and respond well, no matter what their underlying emotions might be." Facing mal-intentioned opponents in practice has strengthened Tom to face whatever comes his way. Tom describes a time when he was working as a hotel manager and an employee's physically impressive and abusive boyfriend stopped at the front desk. "He belligerently demanded to see his girlfriend, and I could tell he wanted to hit somebody. Since I had seen that energy before, I knew what to do." Tom looked the man in the eye and repeated twice that he would not be able to see his girlfriend that day. "In my stature, words, and actions it was clear that he was to leave. I wasn't intimidated or surprised by him. He instantly backed down and left."

And sometimes our battles display a profound core strength that can only be found by touching the deepest depths. "I crawled out of a refrigerator box twenty-four years ago," Jim told me. "I was homeless and killing myself with drugs and alcohol. I don't know why I changed my course that day, but for some reason I took one of the two dimes I had, found a pay phone, and called Alcoholics Anonymous. They told me there was a meeting eight blocks away and asked if I could get there. I could, and on that day I began my road to recovery."

Jim now holds a master's degree in addiction counseling, works with troubled youth, and is married to a school psychologist. He has four children. "I was a Marine in Vietnam and saw some horrible things. I started drinking before I came home and didn't stop. Once I tried to stop drinking by going to a VA hospital and asking for help. They told me that my addiction was a self-inflicted wound. They had no idea what wounds that war created. I don't know how the poor U.S. reservists are going to survive when they come home from Iraq. I'll fight for them if I can."

### Inner Peace

*A Profile in Learning: From a Warrior Attorney*

*My worst opponent? Definitely myself.*

*I was born and raised in a very small Rocky Mountain town. As a family we never really fit in, since our parents had moved there a few years before I was born and had some financial means. This is a tough town where most folks are employed by the local mine or as cowhands or cooks on the surrounding ranches. You'd see families bringing their children during the harsh winter months into the bars, with two-year-olds crawling under the pool table while their parents drank. In my class of ten, many of the girls were pregnant and/or married by the time I graduated. It was a very limiting and unwelcoming place. I like to say that living there was like being a crab in a bucket: one crab tries to climb out, and all the other crabs just pull it back down again.*

*This life has been a hell of an opponent. Add being the youngest child growing up on a ranch fifteen miles outside town with no TV and few friends to visit, and I was really lonely as a kid, desolately lonely. We didn't do sports, which made it all the worse, since the town revolved around football and basketball.*

*Yet growing up here I learned that if you want to make something you simply have to create it. Some great success stories have come out of our town. We had no institutions or corporations that you could plug yourself into, so this path wasn't a way of life that we knew about much less had to fight against. In a way, I had more room to grow, since such a limited environment didn't give me choices to limit me. I've become very comfortable with developing my own version of success. I've learned as a result that any limit is just something I've created in my own mind.*

*I walked away from this place happily twenty years ago. I moved to the East Coast, went to graduate school, and got a law degree. Without much worry I have since started two law firms. Now I return to this little town and drive past the hamburger stand I ate at weekly every summer of my childhood, which sits across the street from the four-bed hospital where I was born, and know that I am home. It defined me and now calls to be better incorporated into who I am today.*

As we grow, we turn away from and say no to all sorts of things. It might be our hometown or a personal trait that we despise. We may turn away from our family of origin. Our enemies can bring us back to what needs to be reintegrated. When we are able to face these opponents and find a place for them within us, we become more whole. Inner peace comes from reintegration and inner expansion. We may fight external battles, but when we turn a "no" into a "maybe" or even a "yes," we may find, as founder of aikido Master Ueshiba counseled, "the only opponent is within."

Matt, sixty-four, practices and teaches an extremely vigorous form of yoga daily and leads a joy-filled life. When I asked him the secret to his vitality and inner peace, he told the story of owning a restaurant in his twenties: "I hired a young buck to make the salads. We had a system for making salads, so as the 'boss,' when I saw the guy making a salad wrong, I confronted him and told him what to do. The waitress intervened saying it was a special request from a customer. Well, I apologized to the guy, who glared back at me and said, 'You keep your mouth shut and stand over there.' So I punched him in the face and sent him flying into the lettuce.

> *What the warrior renounces is anything in his experience that is a barrier between himself and others.*
>
> — TRUNGPA RINPOCHE

"I scared myself, my reaction was so quick. I was and still am clearly my worst opponent. Within a year after that incident, I decided to travel and learn more about who I was." Matt added, "It is all about paying attention. I have found that by constant practice, I observe what appears within. The arrogance, the anger, all the emotions are still there, but I can more consciously choose how to react, and this brings me peace."

Inner peace comes from learning to live within the chaos. At seventy-seven, Phil Heron, once a professional boxer, stagehand, and English professor, has been actively practicing tai chi for thirty years. About opponents he said, "You know, I am very comfortable with instability. It doesn't really bother me. For example, over the years I have had lots of money. Sometimes I have been poor. I like having money better, but I'm okay either way."

Inner peace comes from a brave willingness to look unflinchingly around and within us. This is not an easy business. Think about a painful situation in the world, like the casualties of war. Can you look at the photos of those damaged by land mines and car bombs? Can you stare hatred and misery in the face? Reality can be a tough opponent.

Lynn, who is in her early forties, has Parkinson's disease.

When I met her, I was amazed by how upbeat she was as she labored to walk and to tell her story: "I spent many years fighting this disease, railing against it. One day, I was walking a labyrinth, which is a mazelike path laid into floors of medieval churches. I realized that the meandering path was like my brain. It was also like the disease. Then I realized that this disease and I are one. I don't know how to explain it fully; there was a profound shift. Sure, I'm still going to try to overcome this illness, but I have learned so much from it too. It is part of me."

We find peace when we are equally happy, whether we perceive patience or impatience, anger or kindness. In the Shambhala tradition, we can even come to a place where all is considered perfect and right just as it is. Trungpa Rinpoche adds, "For the true warrior, there is no warfare. This is the idea of being all-victorious. When you are all-victorious, there is nothing to conquer, no fundamental problem or obstacle to overcome... you find that you are genuine and good as you are. In fact, the whole of existence is well-constructed, so that there is very little room for mishaps of any kind." Rumi explains how to welcome and courageously accept all our emotions in his poem "The Guesthouse":

> This being human is a guesthouse.
> Every morning a new arrival.
>
> A joy, a depression, a meanness,
> some momentary awareness comes
> as an unexpected visitor.
>
> Welcome and entertain them all!
> even if they're a crowd of sorrows,
> who violently sweep your house

empty of its furniture,
still, treat each guest honorably.
He may be clearing you out
for some new delight.

The dark thought, the shame, the malice,
Meet them at the door laughing,
And invite them in.

Be grateful for whoever comes,
because each has been sent
as a guide from beyond.

"Trying to be divorced in a good way, that is my definition of a formidable opponent," explained Mary. "It's difficult when you love someone but clearly know that you cannot remain married to him. He is a good, hardworking man, and living together for fifteen years made us both miserable." Since both Mary and her ex-husband's consistent focus is the health and happiness of their two children, she says that her priority is "finding a workable relationship, even if they are divorced." This is far from an easy process. Mary adds, "It is a natural for people to take sides. I see this struggle again and again with my family, friends, and within me. But that doesn't do any of us any good."

On Easter Sunday, Mary invited her ex-husband and his new girlfriend over to brunch. Friends were uncomfortable to find the new couple at the table, but Mary was honestly at peace about the shift in the relationship. "Some think I'm crazy or a saint to do this, but it is self-serving. I know that if I can let our relationships evolve to include these changes, I will be happier. Our children have lots of events ahead, and I want us both to feel comfortable being there."

Mary has found this peace hard-won but worth the pain: "I've seen some very dark places within and can understand now why women take their own lives. But in the dark I find the light. There are moments when the worst of the worst becomes the best of the best. By looking at everything carefully and tenderly, I arrive at a gentle place in the middle where I want the best for him and for me."

## Where Potential Benefits Await

We confront formidable opponents not only individually but as a species. For example, humankind has responded to two world wars, epidemics, and countless other global crises over the past century. Currently, governments and citizens around the world are being called to address the problem of random terrorist attacks. This challenge tears away outdated cultural views and simple comforts. Yet from the loss new questions are now emerging that open us to creating greater unity and safer communities, perhaps as never before.

> *And so in groups where debate is earnest, and especially on great questions of thought, the company become aware of their unity; aware that the thought rises to an equal height in all bosoms, that all have a spiritual property in what was said, as well as the sayer. They all become wiser than they were. It arches over them like a temple, this unity of thought in which every heart beats with nobler sense of power and duty, and thinks and acts with unusual solemnity.*
>
> — RALPH WALDO EMERSON

In 2004 I facilitated some conversations through an international program called The September Project. In small groups, participants between the ages of sixteen and eighty gathered to answer, "What does September 11 mean to us?" Misery and confusion were pervasive, yet diverse issues caused the distress.

"How can I now keep my family safe in a world where terrorists fly into buildings?" was one question that bothered many deeply. Yet, for others, especially those who had traveled internationally, the attacks were not a surprise, and they spoke more about the disbelief at the U.S. response of waging war in Afghanistan, much less in Iraq. These participants struggled with questions like, "How can I face my European friends?" and, "How can I continue to be an American?"

> *With malice toward none, with charity for all, with firmness in the right, as God gives us to see the right, let us . . . achieve and cherish a just and lasting peace among ourselves, and with all nations.*
>
> — ABRAHAM LINCOLN

Others were shocked by the extreme nature of the action. They asked, "How can human beings willingly kill themselves and so many others?" adding, "What would drive me to do the same?" They resisted the human potential for destruction and the terrible conditions that many live with daily. Still others suffered a crisis of faith, descending into pain and existential confusion. "Where was God that morning?" a gentle-hearted man asked an Episcopal priest to his right. "Isn't this all a fight over the definition of God?" was another comment.

These and other questions emerge as the world grapples with diversity, terrorism, and a vastly interconnected economy. The millions of stories that once gave us peace of mind are being eroded, no matter how desperately we might cling to them.

It is now our turn as an international community to identify our opponents, engage, and ask tough questions. I hope that as we serve as everyday warriors in this unknown territory we will each gain increased clarity, connection, strength, and inner peace as a result. In the remainder of the book we will explore techniques that leaders have used over the millennia to creatively meet their adversaries. Using the latest breakthroughs in brain research, in the next chapters we will discover not only what history has shown to be effective but also physiologically why these techniques work.

PART TWO

# An Everyday Warrior's Handbook

*A monk asked, "If on the road one meets a person of the Way, how could one respond to that person with neither words nor silence?" Daopi said, "With kicks and punches."*

— ZEN PARABLE

CHAPTER FIVE

# Engage

*A knowledge of the path cannot be substituted*
*for putting one foot in front of the other.*

— M. C. RICHARDS

*This is a story from the kingdom of Camelot about the Knights of the Round Table. King Arthur sat dining on New Year's Eve with Lady Guinevere and his most trusted knights, Gawain the Good and Agravaine of the Heavy Hand. The halls were filled with jokes and song from good knights clad in red, lovely ladies, and the noblest king the nation had known.*

*No sooner had the first course been served when a huge man rode in on a tremendous green horse. The man too was green of skin and beard. His fine clothing glimmered like emeralds embroidered with inlaid gold. He bore no armor and carried in one hand a sprig of holly, a symbol of peace. In his other hand he held a broad battle-ax of green razor-sharp steel.*

*The Green Knight asked, "Who is the king of these men? I have come to play a game with him." Arthur stepped forward and offered him supper. "I have no interest in dining but offer instead a test for someone who has bold blood and a brash head. I will give you my ax and allow you the first blow. Yet in a year and a day, I must be allowed the same."*

*No one moved. The Green Knight laughed and chided Arthur, "You say you are the living legend? Where is your power and pride now? Are you afraid when no fight is offered?" Arthur, wincing in shame and flushed with anger, stepped forward, demanding the ax. The Green Knight smiled, handed Arthur the ax, and dismounted.*

*Just as Arthur raised the mighty weapon and considered his stroke, Gawain spoke. "Allow me, my lord. My life is little to lose, and it would be improper to have you engage in this mockery." As the knight bowed at his king's feet, Arthur gave Gawain the green ax.*

*Gawain told the knight, "I am Gawain and will bear from you what comes after the blow, but from no other knight alive." The Green Knight smiled and nodded at young Gawain. "You must come find me in one year and a day."*

*Gawain raised the ax, and the Green Knight lifted his curly mane to reveal his verdant neck. Gawain's swift stroke beheaded the Green Knight, and red blood surged from the decapitated body. The Green Knight bent over and picked up his head, mounted his horse, and rode away, calling, "Find me in the Green Chapel."*

*Gawain bore a heavy heart as he hung the ax upon a tapestry, knowing the test had just begun.*

*Eleven months passed, and Gawain started off toward North Wales to find the Green Knight. He donned a shield of bright red gules painted with a pentacle of gold, called the* endless knot, *which reminded him of the five virtues of the knight: friendship, courtesy, a pure heart, generosity, and compassion.*

*Gawain encountered beasts and suffered from great hunger and cold, but could not find the Green Chapel. On Christmas Day, desperate, he prayed to find a place to rest. Looking up he saw a castle suddenly appear, shimmering in the distance.*

*The lord of the castle welcomed Gawain warmly, introducing him to his strikingly beautiful lady of white skin and flushed rose cheeks and to the yellowed old woman who sat beside her. "For sport and to show you are a good guest," the host, Bertilak, said, "let's play a game. For the next three days I will go out hunting with my men, and when I return each evening I will exchange my bounty for anything you manage to acquire in the castle. Then I'll help you find this Green Chapel."*

*Gawain happily agreed.*

*The first morning, the lord hunted a herd of does, while his wife snuck into Gawain's bedchambers hoping to seduce him. Gawain, wishing to stay true to his knightly vows of courtesy and chastity, responded, "I am honored, but this is not to be." The beautiful lady stole one kiss. When Bertilak appeared that evening and asked for his winnings in exchange for venison, Gawain kissed him.*

*On the second day, the lord captured a wild boar, and his wife again tried to woo Gawain. "I am honored, but this is not to be," Gawain replied as this beautiful lady kissed him twice. At dinner Gawain exchanged two kisses with Bertilak for the boar's head.*

*Finally, on the third day, the lord hunted fox. The beautiful lady kissed Gawain three times after trying yet again to embrace the knight. When Gawain again said, "I am honored, but this is not to be," she asked for something to remember him by. Gawain wanted to exchange nothing, until the beauty mentioned that the green and gold silk girdle that she wore around her waist could protect him from dying. Gawain took and hid the girdle that night, giving only three kisses to the host in exchange for a fox skin.*

*On New Year's Day, Gawain rode off with the girdle to seek the Green Knight. At the edge of the forest, a guide sent with him promised not to tell if Gawain decided to give up the quest.*

*Gawain refused, saying, "Good or ill, every man must complete his fate," and bid farewell.*

*Soon after Gawain found a cave partially hidden in tall grasses and called out, "Here I am, do what you will." The huge Green Knight emerged as Gawain bravely presented his neck. The Green Knight then feigned two blows. On a third feint, the Green Knight nicked Gawain's neck, barely drawing blood. "You toy with me, the contract is complete," growled Gawain.*

*The Green Knight then explained, "I am Bertilak, and because you did not honestly exchange all of your winnings on the third day, I had to draw blood on a third blow. You are a noble knight whose life should be spared." He continued, smiling: "The old woman at my table was Morgan le Fay, King Arthur's half-sister. She shifted my appearance into the Green Knight and sent me to Camelot. Is not woman your true enemy?"*

*When Gawain returned to Camelot and shared the tale, he displayed the green girdle and tied it on his left arm, vowing to wear it the rest of his days as a reminder of his failures. In a show of support, all the knights of Camelot bore green girdles on their red-frocked arms.*

Like Gawain, we take on the warrior's role whenever we meet an adversary and wish to serve something greater than ourselves. This tale reminds us that through this journey we will be tested and that the challenges can be terrifying. Yet our sincere commitment can ultimately protect us, and by practicing specific skills we are more apt to succeed.

Although these days not all of us have ready access to formal conflict training, you may have already encountered some of the techniques we will cover in the next four chapters. Some of us have had inspiring sports coaches who provided physical, mental, emotional, and spiritual conditioning strategies to better perform. Others may have found help in confronting vexing problems through studying the spiritual traditions and yoga. Still others may have been taught about being an honorable and courageous leader through military training. Most of us have simply picked up tricks through trial and error that have served us well along the way.

> *The purpose of discipline is to promote freedom. But freedom leads to infinity and infinity is terrifying.*
>
> — HENRY MILLER

The martial arts also codify a heroic warrior philosophy into daily disciplines and techniques. In this chapter we will use the sparring process, which consists of five basic parts, as a useful metaphor for engaging with an opponent:

1. Your shield: a code of conduct
2. The opening bow: beginning well
3. Sparring and competitions: the power of practice
4. The closing bow: honorable closure and integration
5. Proper conditioning: staying strong

This process not only guides our conduct during a difficult conversation, but it centers us so that we may welcome whatever comes to us throughout the day. Just like the mythic warriors of old, we set out to meet our opponents with a strong shield to protect us so we may return home safely from our daily battles.

## Your Shield: A Code of Conduct

Having a set of ethics or ideals that you pledge to stand behind is a distinct characteristic of the principled leader. When one is fighting as part of a team, like the Knights of the Round Table, the group commits to follow a common set of principles both on and off the battlefield. In *The Code of the Warrior*, U.S. Naval Academy professor Shannon French describes a soldier's common code as encompassing "not only how he should interact with his own warrior comrades, but also how he should treat other members of his society, his enemies, and the people he conquers." Our knight Gawain the Good pledged to follow the five virtues of a Round Table knight:

- Friendship
- Courtesy
- A pure heart
- Generosity
- Compassion

Similarly, Joseph Campbell describes the gallant Warrior Way in Japanese mythology as:

- Loyalty with courage
- Veracity
- Self-control
- Benevolence
- A willingness to fully play one's role in the masquerade of life

And from the Lakota tradition we have:

Endurance, cleanliness, strength, purity
Will keep our lives straight
Our actions only for a good purpose.
Our words will be truth.

Only honesty shall come from our interaction
With all things.

Doctors, lawyers, and other professionals also hold to an ethical code such as the Hippocratic Oath and the Model Rules of Professional Conduct. We may develop shared principles through religious membership or through our alliance with an organization like the Rotary or Optimist Club.

Why do we need a code? When we are in positions of power and leadership we can cause harm. When we are in great danger we need guidelines that will keep us clear about our actions. "The code restrains the warrior," explains French. If we, like French's midshipmen students, wield destructive weapons, having a code helps to guide us along the "fine line between warrior and murderer." A study by University of Iowa law professor Mark Osiel cites a young man who, after seeing many of his friends killed, was found by an officer "with his rifle at the head of a Vietnamese woman." The officer simply said, "Marines don't do that," and the young man stepped back and lowered his rifle.

> *There are four bases of sympathy: charity, kind speech, doing a good turn, and treating all alike.*
>
> — BUDDHA

In addition to restraining us, our code protects us. It is no accident that the five-pointed star symbolizing the five virtues of a knight was painted on Gawain's shield. The shield has long been the symbol of one's code of conduct. In ancient times, Spartan mothers, when sending their sons to war, would say, "Come home with your shield or in it," alluding to the critical importance of standing by your ethics in battle, whether you return intact, wounded, or worse.

A common code brings boundaries and honor to a battle. As martial artist Phil Heron states, "The code of a warrior is necessary because without it the opponents are playing different games. Modern warfare is made horrifying by the absence of a code. There is no honor, only death."

In an extensive study on post-traumatic stress disorder among Vietnam War veterans, Jonathon Shay found that those who most suffered from PTSD were involved in wartime experiences that were not only violent but betrayed "what's right." Without their shield to protect them, these men were prone to such miseries as persistent nightmares, addiction, abuse in family relationships, and depression.

Our conflicts will continue to test our shield of ethics and even to pit one principle against another. Gawain struggles with Bertilak and his hostess because he is trying to be both loyal and courteous. In a recent multiple-session workshop, I asked the participants during the first meeting to create a set of ground rules for our sessions together. Their guiding principles included:

- Trying to see from the other's perspective
- Confidentiality
- No political correctness — "just say it"
- No personal attacks
- Honesty
- Enjoyment and having fun

At the beginning of the second session, I reviewed this code of conduct for two new participants. One of these asked, "How can one be honest, avoid political correctness, and not engage in personal attacks?" To her, these ground rules were mutually exclusive. This brought the group to consider the question of how they could be brutally honest and respectful at the same time. Through confrontation, the way we interpret our principles is tested, and we can more deeply appreciate the meaning of our code. The Brahman, in the opening story of this book, appreciates more deeply his ground rule of "caring for even the most pitiful" by the story's end. Caring for even the most pitiful also means caring for himself.

As everyday warriors, we must confront an inescapable test. When we align ourselves with a set of ideals, say, responsibility and honesty, the mirror opposite will also be present. With responsibility comes irresponsibility, and with honesty comes deception. Each has an inherent value. Just as red and green are opposing or complementary colors, crimson-clad Gawain, to reintegrate into his community after his adventure, must wear the emerald girdle. In this act he acknowledges that with high ideals (red symbolizing the heart) comes our basic struggle for survival (green symbolizing nature or the body). By choosing our ethics, we explore their apparent opposites, and through this process we more deeply understand our chosen virtues and ourselves.

> *For equality gives strength, in all things and at all times.*
>
> — MEISTER ECKHART

However, if we do not recognize the natural conflict of opposites that comes with a code of conduct, horrific dichotomies can result. For example, cultures with strong warrior traditions have also unconsciously manifested the extreme opposites of these ideals. The Greek Stoics in the fifth and sixth centuries B.C.E. were a highly disciplined warrior class that believed in controlling all anger, holding high respect for the enemy, and having an impeccable sense of responsibility. Juxtaposed against the Stoics were the Greek hedonists, who killed slaves for sport and delighted in gluttony and sexual perversion. In North America, the Plains Indians warriors would pray with great reverence to the spirit of an animal before a hunt, asking that the animal be sacrificed for the tribe. Once he had killed, the hunter offered more prayers and rituals to respectfully send the spirit to the next world. Meanwhile, this same culture would ritually bring home male prisoners from warring tribes so they could torture them to death.

To keep internal balance while holding to a moral code, Robert A. Johnson, in *Owning Your Own Shadow*, suggests making a "small but conscious gesture" to acknowledge a virtue's opposite. We can use art or writing to acknowledge our impatience after we have spent our day being extremely patient. Johnson tells the story of two women who shared a household in Switzerland. Whoever had some especially good fortune carried out the garbage for a week. If we are going to be a saint, to stay healthy it helps to acknowledge our inner sinner. If we are going to be loyal, recognizing our disloyalty will keep us whole. Creating our own metaphoric green girdles will make us better shield-carrying warriors.

To consider:

- What is my code of conduct?
- How can I safely acknowledge my virtues' opposites?

## The Opening Bow: Beginning Well

Interpersonal conflict can be scary. We worry about getting hurt or putting someone we love at risk. Consciously acknowledging that we are about to enter a confrontation better prepares us to meet an opponent. In aikido, practitioners, when they step on the sparring mat, are taught to begin with a quick bow while looking at their opponent. In the bow you acknowledge that the opponent who stands in front of you is a potential teacher and also one with the capacity to destroy you. The bow says in effect, "Thank you for this opportunity. I am watching you carefully. Teach me."

> *I have never in my life learned anything from any man who agreed with me.*
>
> — DUDLEY FIELD MALONE

The *haka*, or an opening chant that the Maori people of New Zealand recite before going into battle, reflects the tenets of the opening bow. In the *haka* performed by the New Zealand All Blacks professional rugby team while they face the opposing team before each game, they honor the opponent and recognize the transformation the engagement can provide:

*Leader*
KA MATE! KA MATE! (Tis death! Tis death!)
*Chorus*
KA ORA! KA ORA! (Tis life! Tis life!)
*Leader*
KA MATE! KA MATE! (Tis death! Tis death!)
*Chorus*
KA ORA! KA ORA! (Tis life! Tis life!)
TENEI TE TANGATA PU'RU-HURU NA'A NEI TIKI MAI WHAKA-WHITI TE RA!
(Behold! There stands the hairy man who will cause the sun to shine!)
HUPANE! KA-UPANE! A HUPANE! KA-UPANE! (Upward step! Another...! An upward step! Another...!)
WHITI TE RA! (The sun shines!)

The attitude of the opening bow is also contained in the poem by Rumi called "The Chickpea to the Cook":

> A chickpea leaps almost over the rim of the pot
> where it's being boiled.
>
> "Why are you doing this to me?"
>
> The cook knocks him down with the ladle.
>
> "Don't you try to jump out.
> You think I'm torturing you.
> I'm giving you flavor,
> so you can mix with spices and rice
> and be the lovely vitality of a human being.
>
> Remember when you drank rain in the garden.
> That was for this."
>
> Grace first. Sexual pleasure,
> then a boiling new life begins,
> and the Friend has something good to eat.
>
> Eventually the chickpea
> will say to the cook,
> "Boil me some more.
> Hit me with the skimming spoon.
> I can't do this by myself.
>
> I'm like the elephant that dreams of gardens
> back in Hindustan and doesn't pay attention
> to his driver. You're my cook, my driver,
> my way into existence. I love your cooking."

The cook says,
    "I was once like you,
fresh from the ground. Then I boiled in time,
and boiled in the body, two fierce boilings.

My animal soul grew powerful.
I controlled it with practices,
and boiled some more and boiled
once beyond that,
    and became your teacher."

An opening bow does not mean that I like my opponents or even that I invite the fight; it simply recognizes that I need adversaries to evolve. Although I would welcome having everyone adore and agree with me, without opponents I would stagnate and weaken. We need our competitors to improve our businesses. We need our children to push against us to be better parents. We need our partners to disagree so we can find a deeper definition of relationship. When "bowing," I accept that I am about to engage and thus I ready myself. An opponent is not only a great asset but is also potentially dangerous. "Don't kid yourself," one martial artist told me. "I have been struck while bowing."

We can create a symbolic "opening bow" before starting a difficult conversation. I try to begin with a mental picture and an internal checklist. Say my husband and I have been battling about money, and our last conversation ended poorly. The opponent and the conflict are still present and waiting to teach me (darn it!). To "get back on the mat" I visualize myself bowing to him with gratitude. Then I might open the conversation by:

1. Asking if this is a good time and place to talk.
2. Describing where I think we are and where we agree.

3. Making ground rules: What do we need to feel safe enough to talk?
4. Explaining my hopes and what am I committed to.
5. Starting with an open-ended question.

This checklist creates a space in which my opponent and I can meet. In it, I hope to say, "You are important to me. I want us both to feel comfortable so we don't feel a need to hurt each other. Thank you for your willingness to engage."

This kind of gratitude might seem solely altruistic until you realize that gratitude is a powerful countermeasure to debilitating fear. In *What Happy People Know*, Dr. Dan Baker proves that our brain cannot process fear and appreciation at the same time. When we are grateful, we move into our upper cortex and have access to more complex, creative processing. When we are fearful our reptilian brain, where information and decision-making processes are limited, predominates. Gratitude simply allows us to fight more creatively.

Another helpful attitude to incorporate into your opening bow is detachment. We allow for the future to unfold as it will and accept that anything can happen. To be detached means we are actively engaged yet open to new possibilities. Of course we want to protect ourselves, but we honor ourselves and others by admitting that we may not know the best solution to the conflict. Sometimes when we are scared before a confrontation, we become attached to a particular outcome we believe will keep us safe. This constricts our creativity and ability to pay attention. If we become strongly fixated on getting what we want, we can put our shield of ethics

> *We can learn even from our enemies.*
>
> — OVID

and thus ourselves at risk. Instead we need to act from the present moment without the need to control the future. We pay attention to the "here and now," letting our preconceived notions go, and hold to our underlying ethics.

To consider:

- What would you like to remember at the beginning of each difficult confrontation?
- How can you acknowledge fear and secrets so that they don't force your actions?

## Sparring and Competitions: The Power of Practice

When Bertilak's guide takes Gawain to the edge of the forest and promises not to tell if he gives up the quest, Gawain responds, "Good or ill, every man must complete his fate." The knight knows that to live well, he must engage.

To engage well, it helps to practice and hone our skills. In sports, drills and daily training prepare the athlete for peak performance. Those who *practice* the martial arts do just that; they practice their technique again and again. To prepare you to meet your everyday opponents, I suggest two forms of sparring that are particularly helpful when dealing with interpersonal conflict: *finding practice partners* and *using dialogue.*

### *Finding Practice Partners*

You are struggling with your child over curfew and come away frustrated as you reach an impasse. Or you try to implement a new computer system in your healthcare facility, and the doctors won't use it. Before engaging in another frustrating conversation, find a practice partner to pretend to be your opponent — teenager or cardiologist. Find a neutral party who will not be affected adversely if you involve him or her in this conflict. My husband is a good practice partner for our children. In a work situation, it may be an associate who understands the situation and is allied with you so that he does not have to take sides in an existing conflict.

> *Excellence is an art won by training and habituation.*
>
> — ARISTOTLE

Ask your partner to play your adversary to the hilt, to push all your buttons, and to test your arguments. Practice your opening bow and listen to your partner, assuming that you have previously missed something. Use these four guidelines while you fight:

1. Ask open-ended questions.
2. Take yourself lightly.
3. Acknowledge the other's viewpoints.
4. Be honest.

As your partner pretends to be your opponent, he or she may also wish to answer the following questions before sparring to help you gather information:

1. What do you care about most?
2. What scares you?
3. What do you want me to understand?

As you spar, notice where you get caught and lose your momentum. Where does your argument feel weak? Where do you find yourself needing to exaggerate to improve on it? After you finish sparring, ask your partner to provide honest feedback using the following questions as a guide:

1. When did you feel heard?
2. What would you have liked me to say or do?
3. Where am I vulnerable?
4. What are my strengths, and did I use them well?

I have seen "sparring" used successfully by department heads before presenting at major corporate board meetings. Team members play the role of angry and distracted board members and improve the manager's presentation by asking tough questions and looking for weak arguments. By trying to take down their leader in practice, the team strengthens her and prepares her for battle.

Sometimes meeting an adversary under any terms would be impossible given the circumstances, that is, in cases of rape, murder of a family member, or other violent crime. Nevertheless, all parties in the conflict still seek resolution and closure, hoping to benefit from the experience and move on. Representatives of victim and offender rights are working to address this underlying need for resolution. Victim/offender mediation is often used to create closure when all parties are able to meet, discuss the crime, and search for resolutions that may go beyond the court system. However, for cases of violent crimes where meeting with the offender is not possible, a new form of group mediation is emerging.

Pilot programs using surrogates have shown initial signs of lasting success. Facilitators guide meetings in which victims of domestic abuse are brought together with convicted domestic offenders. None of the victims were victims of the abusers in the room. All parties have been through counseling, and the offenders understand the problem of abusive behavior. The nonprofit *Stop It Now!*, based in Massachusetts, has created dialogue circles between surrogate abusers and victims surrounding child abuse. When there is a great imbalance of power, such as in spousal or child abuse, the use of surrogates allows parties to resolve their conflict without having to directly confront their opponents.

> *If we could read the secret history of our enemies, we would find in each man's life a sorrow and a suffering enough to disarm all hostility.*
>
> — HENRY WADSWORTH LONGFELLOW

This process, according to participants, creates enough safety so that each side can learn from the other about the causes of abuse and this difficult relationship without feeling threatened. One female survivor of abuse remarked after using the surrogate process that it was "a journey from hate to hope." A recovering sex offender who took part in a *Stop It Now!* program remarked, "It took the courage of one person to break my cycle of humiliation by confronting me honestly, holding me accountable, and still approaching me with love."

### *Using Dialogue*

*Dialogue* is a Greek word that means "moving through the word." It is an approach to communicating that fosters progress in organizations and individuals. "Dialogue seeks to harness the 'collective intelligence'... of people around you; together we are more aware and smarter than we are on our own," says William Isaacs, founder of the MIT Dialogue Project.

Recently interest in this ancient form of conversation has been growing in corporate and community circles around the world. When using the dialogue technique, people sit in circles and listen in silence while each person speaks. They may pick a theme beforehand, or it might be a monthly gathering where themes and ideas emerge spontaneously. Some use this format to practice communicating about tough subjects. Others use it to resolve group conflict and to work on complex problems. Others learn a great deal just by being present.

> *Now there is cure in coolness and calm, but in heat and passion there can be no cure.*
>
> — MILINDAPANHA

Using dialogue is an opportunity for "cool inquiry," as physicist and systems theorist David Bohm calls it. The format helps to keep emotions from running high so that information can flow freely and the group can act as a coherent whole. It is a discipline that keeps the "fire" of conflict burning under control.

These are the ground rules of using dialogue:

- Everyone has ample time and quiet to speak.
- Listening and learning are prioritized over convincing others of our position.
- Participants ask questions to explore other people's perspectives.
- Very diverse viewpoints can come together in a nonconfrontational way.

Hiring a facilitator who is trained in dialogue techniques might be a first step if you wish to convene a meeting. Once a group is accustomed to the rules and techniques, it can easily self-manage the process. I have included a few dialogue resources in the selected bibliography; below I provide some tips to help you create and maintain a meaningful dialogue:

- *Select a theme* or question to be considered.
- Assign a *timekeeper and recorder* if appropriate.
- *Sit in a circle* to assure equal access to information and equal opportunity to speak.
- See the *other participants as "fascinating strangers"* or holders of the missing pieces of the puzzle you are solving.
- *Check your assumptions.* Practice self-reflection: What do I believe about this situation or the person speaking? Why do I think it is true?
- *Use a "talking piece"* or a single object that is passed around the circle. Only if you are holding the object may you speak.
- *Institute a "no interrupting"* ground rule. The person who is speaking has the floor completely until he or she closes with an agreed-on line like, "I have spoken," "I am finished," or "I open the floor."
- *Make room for silence.* If you want quiet, hold the talking piece or take the floor and don't speak!

The Palestinian/Israeli Parent's Circle consists of members who have suffered through the murder of at least one immediate family member and have pledged not to respond in revenge. The five-hundred-member group is founded on the concept that lack of communication fuels violence on both sides. "Each side has demonized the other," said Aaron Barnea, an Israeli Parent's Circle member, whose son was killed while serving as a soldier in southern Lebanon. "The Israelis think all Palestinians are terrorists who want to slaughter them; the Palestinians think all Jews want them driven from their land and cast into refugee camps. Peace will only be possible when each side throws away these stereotypes." As Palestinian member Nadwa Sarandah explains, "There are always stories behind the story."

The Parent's Circle developed a phone line that facilitates dialogue between Israeli and Palestinian callers. By dialing a four-digit number, "any Israeli can talk to a Palestinian, and any Palestinian can talk to an Israeli." Between October 2002 and May 2005, the Hello Shalom/Hello Salaam project logged over 530,000 calls with over one and a half million minutes of dialogue between the two sides.

Ghazi Brighith, a Palestinian from the West Bank village of Beit Omar, joined the Parent's Circle after his unarmed brother was shot at a checkpoint. One of the first Palestinians to participate in the phone line project, he notes, "The greatest mistake we made was to allow ourselves to stop talking. These days we are under closure. We can't reach Israel. But this is one way we can get around the walls."

The volunteers have been overcome by the success of this experiment. "Once the dialogue starts, people realize how similar they are.... People must make up their own minds about how to create peace," says Aaron. "But we know that dialogue breeds understanding, and this is the first step in any peace process. If we prepare the public, show them both sides want to be proud, independent, and living a normal life, then we've taken a major step towards winning this battle."

> *A man who is swayed by passions may have good enough intentions, may be truthful in word, but he will never find the Truth.*
>
> — GANDHI

His Holiness the Dalai Lama also sees dialogue as a viable alternative to war: "It is my belief that whereas the twentieth century has been a century of war and untold suffering, the twenty-first century should be one of peace and dialogue. As the continued advances in information technology make our world a truly global village, I believe there will come a time when war and armed conflict will be considered an outdated and obsolete method of settling differences among nations and communities."

Although I have used dialogue successfully with adults, I wanted to try it in the home laboratory. In the middle of a recent dinner conversation, I asked the family if we could discuss taking a few days to drive to a favorite Mexican town during spring break. I requested that we use a talking piece and lay down some ground rules. After some grumbling, we chose a metal moose sculpture that was sitting in the center of the dinner table as our talking object. And the fun began.

Since we normally all love to interrupt one another, conflict broke out over who had the moose, who was talking out of turn (all of us), and why we were doing such a terrible exercise. Everyone complained that I had wrecked the dinner conversation and that it was taking forever (we practiced for ten minutes!). Field research can be painful.

When we finally calmed the chaos enough to practice one round of passing the moose to each person, we made some surprising discoveries that make me stand by dialogue as a viable approach. First, each child had a list of things that he or she wanted to say. They grabbed the opportunity of having their family's undivided attention not only to describe what they didn't like about the process but also to move the conversation where they wanted. We received a department store list, a request that an older brother attend an upcoming basketball game, and an explanation of why our eldest loves dinner banter. I realized that one of my children's version of hell is to have his creative expression restricted. "This is like a concentration camp," he added with dramatic flourish. Dialogue is his creative enemy!

This ten-minute experiment transformed our communication patterns for the rest of the evening. Our conversations slowed down, and we stopped interrupting one another. We all listened better, and the process opened a conversation about our collective style that we'd never had before. This exercise also made it clear that dialogue is a tough discipline. It pushes us to listen, to slow down and wait. It restricts our actions, as does any discipline, so that we might refine our skills and improve. Although it may feel difficult at first, like daily exercise, with practice it becomes easier and starts to bear fruit.

Summarizing its place in family communications, our eldest said, "Dialogue makes sense when we are trying to decide something, like if we stay at the beach or drive around, so everyone can have a say. But it doesn't work for normal conversation where I want to ask you a question and have you answer. Then it is really bothersome." In the end, we chose not to drive to the Mexican town, to use dialogue only when we need to decide important issues as a group, and to continue our usual evening chatter the rest of the time.

## The Closing Bow: Honorable Closure and Integration

Many things happen when we fight, and some of them can be pretty lousy. We may come away a confident victor or limp away battered and bruised. We may practice some moves and find ourselves upset or disconcerted. To recover and gain the strength to fight again, we need to first close the fight. Martial artists know that they will return to their opponent soon, if not immediately, and thus, they close each sparring session with a bow. With the closing bow, the opponents return to relative stability and keep

> *If you don't fail now and again, it's a sign you're playing it safe.*
>
> — WOODY ALLEN

open the option of coming together again. And after the bow, they might assess their performance with their teacher or other students.

Like the opening bow, the closing bow expresses gratitude, awareness, and letting go. We can close and integrate by asking ourselves some questions. Just as a coach would review an athlete's performance, the following questions help us see the experience from a more objective perspective:

- What am I grateful for?
- What happened?
- What did I do well, and what will I do differently in the future?
- What do I need to say or do to feel complete?

As with the opening bow, if we close with gratitude we will shift into an attitude of appreciation and thus into the neocortex. From there, we can better integrate the experience, objectively assess our performance, and create closure with the other party.

In researching Vietnam veterans suffering from post-traumatic stress disorder, Dr. Jonathon Shay found that allowing a veteran to fully recount his experience was a key recovery tool. Anthropologist Angeles Arrien, when discussing the importance of closure, suggests recounting our experience as a professional athlete would: "I miscalculated my opponent in the third quarter and executed a poor play," she might explain, and the experience becomes a classroom and not an opportunity to beat herself up. Athletes acknowledge their successes and commit to improving their skills to overcome disappointments. In our story above Gawain demonstrates this refining skill as he returns to Camelot and fully discloses his experience, including his failures. Doing so allows our conscious mind to take in new information and our emotions to reorient. What worked? What didn't? Where am I hurt? What did I learn?

As an example of this process, I was asked to teach as part of a leadership development program. The program director requested that I keep the agenda flexible and listen to the class through their morning discussion and decide what I would teach that afternoon.

As I listened that day, I wrote pages on what might interest the group, and when it came time to teach, overwhelmed by the competing possibilities, I wasn't prepared. Nervous, I started with an exercise and decided to follow the group's feedback to come up with the next topic. This was not an effective approach. I found myself bouncing from concept to concept, trying to please the audience. Some participants left early, and I received mediocre evaluations.

As I recounted my experience to my husband, I was able to better decipher how I had lost the audience's interest. I had to acknowledge my bravery in attempting a new approach, and then I assessed what I would do differently in the future. To fully close, it was also important for me to get the program director's perspective, thank her for the opportunity, and apologize if my miscalculation had caused her any inconvenience.

> *I've always said that in politics, your enemies can't hurt you, but your friends will kill you.*
>
> — ANN RICHARDS

Through closing we work to let past experiences stay in the past so that we have room to process new information. If we are seriously injured, physically, emotionally, creatively, or intellectually, our minds and bodies will continue to process the information in an attempt to fit it within our existing frameworks. Traumatic experiences, such as war, may be so far out of the norm that we cannot find a way to have it make sense. Without a story that tells us this bad thing can happen *and* that we can still be safe, we remain in terror or complete flight-fight reaction. When nothing makes sense, we suffer from PTSD and continue to reexperience the trauma. "Narrative can transform involuntary reexperiencing of traumatic events into memory of the events, thereby reestablishing authority over memory," says Shay. "The task is to remember — rather than relive and reenact — and to grieve." In essence, when you have fought a difficult battle, talk about it when it's over.

However, simple narrative in some cases is not sufficient to move one from a traumatic state and can even exacerbate PTSD symptoms. Recent research shows that other methods, in addition to narrative, may help our brains to release the trauma of a terrible event. In 1987 Dr. Francine Shapiro pioneered eye movement desensitization and reprocessing (EMDR) therapy. In this protocol, a therapist facilitates as the client moves their eyes to the right and left multiple times while thinking of the disturbing event. Through this approach, it appears that the left and right hemispheres of the brain more actively communicate to process the trauma, allowing fear to recede.

> *Stretch your arms and take hold the cloth of your clothes with both hands. The cure for pain is in the pain. Good and bad are mixed. If you don't have both, you don't belong with us.*
>
> — RUMI

A simple closing exercise that seems to stimulate this type of brain processing is the "butterfly hug." Cross your arms so that your left hand rests on your right upper arm and your right hand rests on your left upper arm. Now, thinking about the event, gently tap your right arm once with your left hand, and then tap your left arm with your right hand. Alternate gently tapping your arms, right and left. This exercise has been shown to be successful in helping children in Nicaraguan, Mexican, and Kosovar refugee camps recover from trauma. By creating dual-hemisphere stimulation, these exercises can calm and provide new perspective to any disturbing experience.

To consider:

- In which of my contests have I neglected to do a closing bow?
- Where do I still need to close with myself?

## Proper Conditioning: Staying Strong

To enable us to fight over long periods of time, heroic warrior traditions include strict conditioning. Athletes, for example, are given an exercise regimen and drills to practice. They must eat a nutritious diet and get ample sleep. They are given time to rest and recover. Their practice schedule assures that when they compete they are fully ready.

When I coach corporate and nonprofit managers, I see their roles as matching those of the warrior. They seek bravely to serve their community and face great challenges and adversaries each day. They want to be strong and versatile to accomplish great goals. Some of the amazing projects they wish to accomplish are multiyear battles. Yet these managers, like so many of us, fail to recognize that we all require daily conditioning to fight well. Too often sleep is given over to catching up on email. Breakfast and lunch are sporadically eaten on the run. We make little room in our day for exercise and for downtime to recharge our batteries. When coaching, my mantra has become, "Exercise, nutrition, rest, and recovery."

Can you imagine being a professional athlete and not exercising, eating well, and resting? Yet how often do we embark on our own competitions without these basics? We often become our own worst enemies by not caring for the warrior within. We need our minds and hearts operating at top capacity for the long haul, and there are simple steps we can take to give ourselves a fighting chance. My husband likes to call self-care "taking your MEDS," or remembering to include: Meditation, Exercise, a healthy Diet, and ample Sleep. Our brains are our most important resources when we are confronting challenges, and recent research shows that these MEDS provide the brain the nutrients and recovery needed to function at top form. In the next chapter, we will also discuss the important benefits of meditation. As John Ratey states, "Physical and mental exercise, proper nutrition, and adequate sleep will help anyone gain cognitive clarity and emotional stability." Ratey provides some other fun facts to help keep us motivated to take our MEDS:

- Exercise increases the production of our neurotransmitters, which support mood regulation, anxiety control, and the capacity to deal with stress.
- Older men who stay in shape score better on mental tests, sometimes equal to men thirty to forty years their junior.
- Even minor deficiencies in necessary vitamins and minerals can promote personality and mood changes, impaired reasoning, and aggressiveness.
- Conditions like memory loss, depression, and confusion once thought connected to aging are also indicators of a poor diet.

- Israeli researchers Avi Karni and Dov Sagi have shown that interrupting REM sleep sixty times a night will completely block learning. Sleep is essential to organizing information and forming lasting memories.

> *I can like my fellow men only when I am at my peak of vigor and am not depressed. To be in this condition I must keep my body trimmed. Any revolution must begin here in my body.*
>
> — CARLOS CASTANEDA

Self-care and being aware of our physical state is an ongoing process. As parents or leaders, we help children and others to recognize the need for balance and to choose the appropriate time to engage. It can take a few tactical errors before we realize that we are strongest and most creative after a good night's sleep and a nutritious meal. In my case, it took becoming a mother of three before I realized how precariously balanced I am before dinner. When tired and hungry, I must remind myself that to fight fair I must take care of myself first.

What throws you off? Depending on our physiology and our personalities, we may need not only food, exercise, and rest, but also time, space, and additional information. Watch what helps you move under stress. Is it a break, a meal, or the acknowledgment by another of your situation? Your self-awareness and care will serve everyone involved.

Often we wait till we're on vacation to take care of ourselves. I suggest that we see sleep, proper nutrition, and downtime as required components of our daily lives. As a result, we will become more productive and need less total time to complete our work. When our minds and bodies are well conditioned we can follow the Taoist adage "Do without doing and everything gets done."

To consider:

- When am I precariously balanced?
- What are three steps I can take to improve my self-care habits this week?

Remembering the five parts of engaging with an opponent — grab shield, open, engage, close, and recover — whenever an opponent appears can both ground and empower us to respond. Being a principled leader is a balancing act. We must weigh our own needs with those of our community. We will need to balance between listening and speaking, inquiry and advocacy. We will need to include both action and time for reflection, and we will value both giving and receiving. The Tibetan Shambhala tradition describes this constant dual focus as the warrior carrying *insight* in one hand and *compassion* in the other into each battle. Both are equally necessary and improve our capabilities as we face our opponents. In the next two chapters, we will explore techniques to sharpen our minds and then condition our hearts so we may lead and respond in a balanced and productive manner, regardless of the situation.

> *Becoming real is more a process of letting go than it is the effort of becoming. I don't really have to become myself, although at times I feel this way. I already am what I am. And that is both the simplest and the hardest thing for me to realize.*
>
> — HUGH PRATHER

CHAPTER SIX

# Sharpen the Mind

*I thank God for my handicaps, for, through them,*
*I have found myself, my work, and my God.*

— HELEN KELLER

*From Korea comes a story about a young woman, Yun Ok, whose husband returned home after three years of fighting in a terrible war. Her husband hardly spoke with her, and when he did he was terribly rough. He hated the food she made and didn't seem to hear anything she said. When she spied on him at his work, she would find him alone, sitting on a hill, looking out at the rice fields. This was not the gentle and loving man who had left Yun Ok to go to war.*

*Yun Ok went to a mountain hermit who was known for making charms and magic potions and told him of her worries. "This sometimes happens when young men return from wars," acknowledged the hermit.*

*"Make a potion to bring my husband back," she said.*

*"Come back in three days," said the sage.*

*Three days later Yun Ok returned, and the hermit said, "Your potion can be made. Bring me the whisker from a living tiger, and I will give you what you need."*

*Yun Ok was stunned. "A whisker of a living tiger, how will I do that?"*

*"If the potion is important enough, you will succeed," the hermit replied and returned to his hut.*

*Yun Ok went home and thought about how she would get the tiger whisker. One night she crept out of the house with a bowl of rice and meat sauce in her hand and headed to a cave where a tiger was reported to live. Standing far from the cave she called to the tiger to come eat, but no one came.*

*The next night Yun Ok went to the tiger's cave, this time standing a bit closer and offered the food. Each night that followed, she moved a few steps closer with a bowl of food in hand. And bit by bit the tiger in the cave grew accustomed to her presence.*

*One night Yun Ok was a few steps from the cave when the tiger walked toward her, and they stood looking at one another. The next few nights they moved step by step closer until they looked into each other's eyes in the moonlight. Yun Ok spoke soothingly to the tiger. That very next night, after looking in Yun Ok's eyes, the tiger ate the food she carried.*

*Soon, the tiger would wait for Yun Ok on the trail. Yun Ok could now pet the tiger. Nearly six months had passed, when Yun Ok gently spoke, "Dear tiger, I must snip one of your whiskers. Please do not be angry with me."*

*And Yun Ok gently cut a single whisker.*

*The tiger did not anger, and with joy the young wife ran down the trail.*

*The very next morning, Yun Ok returned to the hermit, pleading, "Here is the whisker. Make my husband loving and gentle again!"*

*The hermit slowly examined the whisker, asking her all the steps she had taken to get it. When satisfied, he turned and threw it in the fire.*

*"What have you done? How are you going to make a potion?" Yun Ok cried. "I want my husband back!"*

*"The potion is complete. Just as you have tamed the tiger, bring your husband back," the hermit replied and sent the woman home.*

Yun Ok demonstrates the keen observation skills and patience required of us as everyday warriors. We see through her constancy of practice that our minds too can be disciplined to handle the dangers and commitments of leadership.

In this chapter we will explore four universal practices that heighten our warrior capabilities by training the mind: cultivating the observing eye, creating space through meditation, blending with our opponents, and fostering witness consciousness.

## Cultivating the Observing Eye

It has been a sunny and unseasonably warm January week as I write this chapter. My friends say things like, "I'm not comfortable with this," "When will we get more snow? I'm worried about fires this summer," and, "Isn't this marvelous?"

We naturally take in information like the warm weather and offer an opinion. We judge it good or bad, and depending on one's perspective, it creates worry or calm. Our perceptions then drive our decisions. Our conclusions distract us. We go inward to judge not only the situation but ourselves: "Is it because we are all driving SUVs that we are having this weather?"

In comparison, to heighten awareness, martial artists, scientists, and religious contemplatives around the world are trained to solely observe without jumping to conclusions. As one of the classic Eastern texts on battle, *The Book of Five Rings*, states, "Observation and perception are two separate things; the observing eye is stronger, the perceiving eye is weaker. A specialty of martial arts is to see that which is far away closely and to see that which is nearby from a distance. . . . It is essential to see both sides without moving the eyeballs."

With this method we are taught to observe what we see, feel, hear, or smell without perceiving it as good or bad. Initiates in these traditions are taught to stay in the present so that they can gather more information and respond. In a real battle this kind of focused observation can increase my chances for survival. If a sword is coming toward my face, there is no time for "Is this good or bad?" "I am not good at this," or "I remember when." A sword is coming, I meet the sword. You are lunging, I respond. I don't judge the situation, you, or my performance. There can be time for judgment later.

As we cultivate an observing eye, we open ourselves to new information. Systems theory shows that those systems that are the most open to information coming in from their surrounding environment are the most vital. If we choose to close ourselves off from disturbances and seek only equilibrium, we position ourselves for fragility. When I struggle with an opponent and have some time, I practice observing by writing down everything I can about the situation. What do I see? What am I feeling? What do I smell, taste, notice? Just write. No judgment, just gather. What do I observe about my opponent? What does my opponent believe?

> *Creativity comes from accepting that you're not safe, from being absolutely aware, and from letting go of control. It's a matter of seeing everything — even when you want to shut your eyes.*
>
> — MADELEINE L'ENGLE

Through cultivating the observing eye we can further develop our neocortex and expand our perspective. In *A User's*

*Guide to the Brain*, John Ratey explains, "Extra use means extra cortex. The lesson... is that ongoing perception reshapes the ongoing brain. Practice makes new brain."

We must also observe our assumptions. As I extend my right hand, you will probably guess that you too should extend your right hand to shake mine. You would make the *assumption* that I am greeting you and would have an *expectation* that once we were done shaking hands we would then proceed to the next phase of social interaction, talking with each other.

Yet assumptions and expectations are dirty words in many circles. One cultural story has it that to have expectations is to be constantly disappointed. However, assumptions are our shortcuts to answers, and some expectations must come with relationships. What if I could never expect that a green light meant "go" and questioned that at every stoplight? If you were driving behind me, you'd assume I was an idiot!

Our assumptions drive our actions, yet we are often unconscious of them. For example, heading off on a business trip, I saw my friend Felicia sitting in the airport lounge surrounded by packages and a cane. I remembered she had once told me that she struggled with differing leg lengths, and I assumed that a resulting problem had flared up. I asked, "What happened? Are you okay?" Felicia smiled, indicating the packages and cane and said, "I'm off to a painting class. We hang canes off the edge of our canvases to track if our arms are in the right position."

Then we boarded the plane. I was seated in front of a couple I knew peripherally. We were flying to Minneapolis, where I had previously seen them walking through the airport and had filed away somehow that this was their hometown. "Where are you going?" I asked. They replied, "To visit our grandchild." Well, jumping to conclusions, I decided their child must still be living in Minneapolis. "Where in the Cities does your son live?" I then asked. "Boston, Minneapolis," the husband smartly replied. I love this part. I said, "I don't know that town; it must be small and outside the city?" "No, our child lives in Boston, Massachusetts," he laughed. I was at least zero for two on my assumptions that morning.

Assumptions are necessary survival tools, since they create shortcuts to decisions. Yet they also lead us to premature judgment. Perceptions like "He's a creep" or "She doesn't understand the situation" close us off to gathering important information and clutter our minds with opinions. David Bohm, in his studies on effective dialogue, suggested that we "suspend" our assumptions: "Assumptions will come up . . . the natural response might be to get angry, or get excited, or to react in some other way. But suppose you suspend that activity. You may not even have known that you had an assumption. . . . That's all part of the observation, the suspension. You become familiar with how thought works."

When we hold all the contradicting pieces of information within us without judgment, new answers or expanded perceptions can emerge. In the opposites we find win-win solutions that no one thought possible: ways that companies can be both profitable and benefit the environment or how Yun Ok's marriage can once again thrive after war. As Kakuzo Okakura describes in *The Book of Tea*, "Truth can only be reached by the comprehension of opposites." And as we see in the story of Yun Ok, careful observation takes time. It is a step-by-step process that can bring us to peace with our tigers.

Meanwhile, we are wired to perceive and jump to conclusions. Our ability to perceive danger and various patterns is a powerful tool. As Einstein once said, "If the researcher went about his work without a preconceived opinion, how should he be able at all to select out those facts from the immense abundance of the most complex experience . . . to permit the lawful connections to be evident?" We need to be able to perceive. To cultivate an observing eye, we just need to learn not to turn on the perceiving mind too quickly and prematurely jump to conclusions. It is a practice of patience, of simply observing and asking questions. Begin by picking a moment each day and write down all you observe. Pretend you are a scientist observing an important experiment, a truly valuable experiment called your life.

## ♡ Creating Space through Meditation

With all the information streaming around us, it is no surprise that our minds get cluttered and our emotions get thrown off-kilter throughout the day. The practice of daily meditation, or sitting quietly with one's mind empty, helps us to counteract data overload by cleaning out the excess and calming us so that we can see more clearly. It allows our minds to recoup and process all the stimuli with which we have been bombarded. It creates mental space. Ratey adds, "Our brains are not infinite. They run out of space, run out of gas, as it were. If the brain is busy trying to filter uncomfortable and frustrating noise, worries, or other concerns, there is less 'brain stuff' available for perceiving."

> *Wisdom comes out in the village of infinite nothingness; spirituality is found in the realm of unfathomability.*
>
> — FA-YEN

Meditation is a powerful method of coping with life's challenges and difficult people. Although some perceive it as a daunting or boring practice that only religious people do, because of its effects on mental and physical health, brain processing, and athletic performance it has garnered keen interest in the sports, medical, and personal development fields. Studies have shown that meditation lowers our heart rates, reduces blood flow and pressure, and lowers the metabolism. These results have been found to provide anxiety sufferers with a sense of peace without medication, to reduce the incidence of migraine headaches, and to soothe chronic pain. The meditative state can counteract the flight-fight response to bring calm and focus during stressful situations.

> *Meditation is a process of lightening up, of trusting the basic goodness of what we have and who we are, and of realizing that any wisdom that exists, exists in what we already have. . . . The key is to wake up, to become more alert, more inquisitive and curious about ourselves.*
>
> — PEMA CHÖDRÖN

Meditation also appears to boost our immunity. The findings of one study show that "women who meditate and use guided imagery have higher levels of the immune cells known to combat tumors in the breast." And University of Wisconsin researcher Richard Davidson tested meditation's effect on the immune system by giving flu shots to a group of volunteers from a high-tech company. A control group received eight weeks of meditation training. By the study's completion, the meditators showed a healthier immune response to the flu than those who received only the immunization shot.

We can acquire the benefits of meditation as soon as we begin to practice it. We continue to grow new neurons throughout our adult lives; our brains possess a kind of *neuroplasticity*. At the E. M. Keck Laboratory for Functional Brain Imaging and Behavior in Madison, Wisconsin, neuroscientist Richard Davidson is working to prove that we can reprogram our minds through meditation to overcome anger, anxiety, and depression and to alleviate the need for pharmacological solutions. Meditation appears to develop the left prefrontal lobe, which regulates positive emotion.

> *No trumpets sound when the important decisions of our life are made. Destiny is made known silently.*
>
> — AGNES DE MILLE

To meditate all you need is to sit quietly somewhere for a set period of time, say ten to forty minutes daily, and let your mind rest. It sounds simple, but it can actually be a tough daily discipline. To help you start, I offer the following suggestions derived from both expert advice and my own efforts to integrate meditation into daily life.

### *Create a Routine*

1. Create a meditation space. It can be as simple as a cushion in the corner of your bedroom or a full meditation room with a pleasing, peaceful decor.
2. Make a commitment to try the practice for a set period of time and tell someone you respect about this commitment. "I will practice twenty minutes of seated meditation daily for the next three months," might be a declaration. My teachers have suggested sixty to one hundred days as a minimum commitment to make a habit stick.
3. If you miss a day, go back to the cushion the next.
4. Create a ritual that your body will become as accustomed to as your morning cup of coffee. An example would be to turn off the lights, light a candle, sit in the same spot, or wrap yourself in a blanket. The ritual settles us into the practice and into the desired mental state more quickly.

*Make It Comfortable*

1. Buy yourself a meditation cushion or use a chair on which you can easily sit upright.
2. Stretch or exercise a little before sitting.
3. Find a quiet place free of distractions, and turn off the phone.
4. Each day will be different. If you are tired or agitated before beginning, create bridges to the cushion, like taking a cool shower or reading a favorite poet.

*Learn to Sit*

1. Keep your spine straight, with your chin tucked in slightly and your jaw relaxed.
2. Rest your hands on your knees or in your lap.
3. Close your eyes or leave your eyes half-closed gazing toward the floor.
4. Listen to your breathing, clearing your mind of all thoughts.
5. As thoughts and emotions arise, acknowledge them: "That is a thought" or "That is anger," and let them move through.
6. When thoughts and emotions do carry you away, return to your breath.

*Helpful Tools for the Beginner*

1. When breathing, repeat a positive phrase, like "thank you," "I am well," or "all is well."

2. Count your breaths.
3. Set a timer so you don't keep looking at the clock.
4. Use beads to count your breaths and measure time. Move from bead to bead with each in-out breath cycle. A rosary, found at most Christian supply stores, and Buddhist *mala* beads serve well. In the bibliography I have included a book about making your own prayer beads. With 108 beads and a few "oops, I'm off in thoughtland" deviations, one trip around helps keep you on the cushion for a good fifteen minutes.

Meditation not only strengthens but softens us as well. It has often helped me win the game I call my "internal hide-and-seek." For example, I might wake up feeling lousy. When I started meditating seriously, I couldn't name the feeling, it was just this edgy state that I hated. If I observed my actions, I found that it caused me to want to control my children's every movement. Since I had committed to a teacher that I highly respect to do seated meditation for a year, when those edgy mornings came, I still went to my cushion, even though it was the last thing I wanted to do.

> *Half an hour's meditation each day is essential, except when you are busy. Then a full hour is needed.*
>
> — ST. FRANCIS DE SALES

As I sat, first fighting the feeling, I would make lists of what I wanted to do that day or think about the dream I had the night before. Then my thoughts would clear, and I would settle in. Soon I would notice the emotion and say to myself, "I'm miserable." If I could just let myself feel the sadness or even the depression that appeared, it would transform. Day after day, I became more comfortable with letting myself be miserable, afraid, or depressed, and I got better at letting everyone else in the house be just as they were. I felt much better about my interactions with others when I was able to be gentler with myself.

There are still days when I want to run and hide and I am not interested in meditating. Yet when I do meditate, I am constantly amazed at how it helps me locate myself on both my inner and external battlefields. I gain not only some peace of mind but also new perspective on my challenges.

## Blending with Our Opponents

Our fighting style determines how well we learn. When I interviewed martial artists from different traditions, including aikido, tae kwon do, and karate, they all talked of "blending with your opponent." As one thirty-year tai chi practitioner explained, "Merging with your opponent is not a metaphor, it is a fact. You want to be so connected with the energy of your opponent that when his arm rises yours moves to meet his without your thinking."

What is blending or merging? Have you noticed how tiny martial artists can throw opponents twice their size or weight? Adversaries bring with them a force, a kind of energy. We can take that energy within us and use it. Sometimes martial artists will use their opponent's force to bring their adversary to the ground and immobilize him. Other times it can be directed so we can see in new directions. Using force brought by our opponent to move makes a fight a cocreated dance.

To practice blending, I use an exercise that comes from master aikido instructor Tom Crum, author of *The Magic of Conflict*:

- Find a partner.
- Have her try to bend your arm while you attempt to be strong and keep it straight out in front of you. Observe how you might make a fist and strain against her. Notice how this mode of fighting is often painful!
- Next, try not resisting at all. Feel how your arm flops around as you completely give up. Notice how ineffective this reaction to conflict can be.
- Now try blending with your opponent's energy. First locate your physical center by placing your hand about two inches below your navel. Your center (also called primary *don tien*, *chi*, or *banda*) is considered your main energy source in the martial arts and yoga.
- Breathe into this spot, pretending to bring all your energy to your center. Breathe any stress, thoughts, or constriction down into this spot.
- Now raise your arm again, with fingers extended, and pretend that it is a fire hose bringing all your energy, like water, from your center through your arm and sending it out past any wall that may be in front of you. Imagine that you are "spraying" this energy from your source through your extended arm with a blast like a fire hose would provide. Your arm becomes unbendable as it is filled with this strong flow.
- As your opponent tries to bend your arm, take all the energy she is giving you through your arm down into your center. Breathe it all in, and then spray this too out through your arm.

In the first two steps, resistance and total surrender, we do not accept our opponent's energy; we push it away or ignore it. But then we consciously bring in this energy and release it.

Blending is learning. We must first take in new information and notice our observations and perceptions. We practice acceptance. Yun Ok must accept that the tiger is a tiger and thus comes with certain attributes. She also recognizes that her husband has been traumatized by war. In this acceptance or "breathing in" of what is, we gain energy that can be used in whatever manner we see fit. It is active engagement with what is occurring around us. In blending we meet an opposing force, engage with it by taking it in, and then respond.

The Buddhist tradition teaches *tong len* to learn merging. This is a breathing method that can be practiced anytime we wish to run away from or resist our adversary. With *tong len* we breathe in what we do not like, and exhale what we want to bring to the world. Say you are in the grocery store and see a mother screaming at a child. You would breathe in, saying, "impatience" or "cruelty" and then breathe out saying, "peace and hope." Or you look at the front page of the newspaper and breathe in, saying, "crime" and breathe out saying, "kindness." Breathe in what you don't like, accept it, and breathe out how you wish to respond.

We can also blend with our internal opponents to become calmer and more powerful. Author and lecturer Tara Brach practices "radical acceptance" when facing inner opponents. We might not want to feel afraid, angry, or inadequate, so we either fight against these feelings, or we totally surrender and drown in them. Radical acceptance rises from the Buddhist Vipassana (translated as "to see clearly" from Pali) meditation system. Brach counsels that we accept what is within us without judgment. When we are struggling internally, we simply name it and let it be.

As I write today, I jot down my inner banter as an example: I am afraid that I won't explain this topic well or have enough time to finish before the deadline. I am worried that I am not being present enough to my children, and I am judging myself too harshly. I love the beautiful warm day and I want to get my windows washed. I'm nervous, happy to be alive, feeling silly writing this down, hoping the dogs don't pee on the rug, and still nervous. My heart is tight, my throat a bit constricted, I feel trusting yet scared. Now my heart feels better. I'm thankful to see the moon setting huge and yellow behind a blue mountain with a pink sky this morning and that my family invited me out to see it. I worry I am missing life as I focus on projects like this. I don't want to waste it. Life is so precious and short, I don't want to die and miss any of it, ever....

Sometimes when I allow myself to view some of my regrets and worries, I burst into tears and collapse with sorrow. This is my version of the flip-flopping arm as I lay on my back in submission to my inner adversaries. Other times, I will try to ignore my feelings and attempt to forge ahead. This approach is not very successful either; these feelings sneak through anyway when I am sleeping or tired.

Yet with *tong len* and radical acceptance, if we name what we see and accept it as it is, we can *choose* how to respond. I realized after writing the above list that I wanted to go for a walk, enjoy this uncharacteristically warm January day, and tell my children that I love them. We stop running internally (or at least we slow down a bit!). Depending on our ability to accept what is, fear, worries, and even death become as much allies as they are enemies.

Blending does not mean we agree with or approve of what comes at us. It is simply a process of gathering information and recognizing it as it is. We open ourselves to see what is around and within us. Critical information often passes us like a slinking dog that bites us from behind later. By turning down the volume on our judgments and cultivating observation skills, we open ourselves to new insights and evolution.

## Fostering Witness Consciousness

Many traditions hold that opponents are sent to teach us specific things. We may need to wake up to a situation that does not serve us or that demonstrates the limitations of our beliefs. Paradoxically, our adversaries obstruct our path so we can see more clearly; they turn us to another, safer road.

Another worldview holds that reality is created by a set of invisible stories that recruit participants. Each drama comes with a question wishing to be answered. Sometimes we are willing actors, and other times we find ourselves surprised to be in the midst of a surreal drama. Yun Ok had been unhappily called into a story to be a hero and to answer the question, "How do we bring our loved ones fully home after war?"

Seeing our opponents as messengers or ourselves as actors fosters an attitude of detachment. We mentally step back to observe our lives while we participate. We act in the play and watch it at the same time. The yogic tradition calls this attitude "witness consciousness." When in a difficult position, to stay with it, we back up mentally to notice how we are feeling, what hurts, if we are breathing, and so on. It may be helpful to see this as moving our perspective outside our

> *Be patient toward all that is unsolved in your heart and try to love the questions themselves. . . . Do not now seek the answers, which cannot be given to you because you will not be able to live them. And the point is, to live everything. Live the questions now. Perhaps you will then gradually, without noticing it, live along some distant day into the answer.*
>
> — RAINER MARIA RILKE

bodies and looking at ourselves from above. "Look how worried I am" or, "I'm really tired" might be some of the realizations that come to us when we shift to a more detached place.

Through witness consciousness, you can stay with a difficult situation longer and learn from it. We distance our egos a bit from the problem. In *Romancing the Shadow*, Connie Zweig and Steven Wolf explain that when tough situations or people appear, we can draw on the mythic warrior Odysseus's method of confronting the sirens. After plugging the ears of all his shipmates so they would not be driven crazy, Odysseus was strapped to the mast so he could fully witness the sirens' calls. Grounded, tied to his reality, he then could directly confront their tactics but not be drawn in to them.

> *When a man realizes*
> *He is neither the doer*
> *nor the enjoyer,*
> *The ripples of his mind*
> *are stilled.*
>
> — ASHTAVAKRA GITA 18:51

Using the observing eye, meditation, and blending techniques described above, we too can ground and separate ourselves to see more clearly. We can recognize that we all play roles in the "masquerade of life" by backing up and asking, What part have I picked to play today? Who has joined me? What is the underlying theme of our production?

I unwittingly experienced the insight that comes with witness consciousness one Sunday last January. Our small town has been privy to a dissemination of literature from a "pro-White" organization called the National Alliance. The brochures left on doorsteps have raised deep concern within the community and fear among those who have racially and religiously diverse families.

To commemorate Martin Luther King Jr.'s birthday, over two thousand people gathered for a diversity march and rally. I was asked to be a peacekeeper, or one who could stand between the marchers and the National Alliance who were holding a counterdemonstration on the courthouse steps. With an orange plastic armband denoting my role, I walked down Main Street with the crowd a half mile to the courthouse, which faced the auditorium where the diversity rally was scheduled.

> *Courage is fear holding on a minute longer.*
>
> — THOMAS FULLER

As an official peacekeeper I squared my shoulders as I walked, on the lookout for trouble. I noticed a young man with a shaved head in front of me wearing tight jeans, army boots, and a jean jacket sporting patches with the names of punk and rock bands like "4Skins." He carried a cane, which he didn't seem to need. He walked with another man who had dyed-black hair, was wearing chains, and had a face full of piercings. My antennae were up, but as I watched their relaxed exchanges, I decided that both appeared to feel at home as they strolled into the center of the pro-diversity crowd.

When we came to the courthouse, the sea of walkers slowed to a crawl as the marchers looked toward the "enemy." About a dozen young men and two twenty-something women held signs with messages like "Love your race" and "Not in our town" and that sported symbols banning homosexuality and communism. Those of us wearing orange armbands moved between the marchers and the courthouse demonstrators asking the marchers to keep moving toward the auditorium and not to engage. Most gawked and raised their diversity signs but moved on.

Then, a group of mostly young men, led by the fellow with the cane who had walked ahead of me, began to form out of the pro-diversity folks in front of the peacekeepers. To the outside eye, the newly collected team of men was a tough, ready-to-fight faction. They put bandannas over their faces and raised signs that said things like "No hate in our town" and "The only way to get rid of Nazis is to kick them out" or had large swastikas crossed out. They glared at the pro-White group, took pictures of them, and refused to move from their spot in the street. I asked one of my more hip compatriots who this group of twenty staring down the pro-White opponents was. She explained that they were "skinheads for peace."

For the next fifteen minutes, I stood between these two groups in a standing mediation of sorts. The other peacekeepers and I asked each side not to engage or to stop trading insults, just like one does across the mediation table when violence looks imminent. Since there were police around us and the few National Alliance folks seemed more interested in talking to the media than in fighting, I wasn't afraid and allowed myself to back up and be fascinated by the conflict. I had not wanted to march, even though many of my friends had called me specifically to attend. But the opportunity to stand between the two groups as a peacemaker seemed like research for this book and an opportunity to look at the question of difference.

> *Everything works out in the end. If it hasn't worked out, it's not the end.*
>
> — UNKNOWN

These two groups were demographically so similar in their numbers, gender, and age makeup with their signage and their chants of "not in our town." Even their hate of the other's message felt the same as I stood between them. They were predominantly young men raring for battle, standing up straight and bold.

In the midst of this battle, I just couldn't get over the irony of the greater diversity march's theme: "All are welcome . . . except those we don't agree with." It reminded me of a statement I once made to my daughter as we passed a very conservative church in town that condemns all traditions that do not match theirs. I had burst out, "I hate people who hate people." My daughter sat for a while in silence. Then she asked tentatively, "So you hate yourself?" I had to laugh and marvel at her assessment.

Later, in the auditorium, two new opposing sides emerged. The first speaker was Henrietta Mann, the first endowed chair of the Native American Studies program at Montana State University. She opened with a prayer spoken first in Cheyenne then in English:

> Ma'heo'o, Great One, Holy Mystery, All Spirit who lives in all things and who appears in many ways: hear me as I humbly offer this prayer to you, to the sacred powers of the four directions, and to the Earth who loves, nourishes, supports, and sustains us on this human journey we travel together....
>
> Ma'heo'o, I ask you to bless all who live within this community...Let us always remember to celebrate and respect diversity. Let us always remember our kinship to one another....
>
> Ma'heo'o, today, as we stand within this circle, teach us to live in proper relationship with all that exists in your expansive creation: the sun, moon, stars, air, earth, water, light, and *with all our relations.*

Yet the speakers who followed Henrietta — gracious middle-aged folks — provided a message very similar to that of all the young men outside. Presenter after presenter said that no one who hates others was welcome in our community. I finally understood why I had not wanted to come. Henrietta described the inclusive view that I strive to stand for. Meanwhile, the protestors on both sides had mirrored a position of exclusivity that I don't like within myself in which we "hate people who hate people."

> *A man cannot be too careful in the choice of his enemies.*
>
> — OSCAR WILDE

Let's frame the drama as a question: How can we protect

what we value *and* welcome opponents in our community? Where is the win-win? These are the foundational questions of any community between exclusivity and inclusivity.

> *Out of Supreme love*
> *they swallow up each other*
> *But separate again*
> *for the joy of being two.*
>
> *They are not completely the same*
> *but neither are they different.*
> *No one can tell exactly*
> *what they are.*
>
> — JNANESHWAR (OR JNANADEVA)

Who were the opponents in the battle that day? It just depends on how we choose to cut it. I am reminded of Shakespeare's *A Midsummer Night's Dream*, where through the work of fairies, lovers suddenly hate each other and become infatuated with others, only to wake up back in love again with those they once hated. This enemy-making is fickle business, and we are capricious souls. In the group of thousands, depending on how we look at it, enemies become allies and then turn into neutral parties. There was the battle of the liberals versus the neo-Nazis. Or was it a fight between those who believe in categorizing people as demons versus those who believe that we are all humans deserving of equal treatment? Maybe it was a portrait of humankind's constant struggle between trying to accept this mysterious world as it is and wanting to create change as the activists on both sides mirrored.

Pick the question, and then draw new battle lines. The day of the march, I could choose among lots of potential actors for whatever drama or comedy I wanted to create. We create opponents so we can learn from them. It is in our questions and the recognition that we choose to create enemies that we can find heightened awareness. In many ways every person's story is very similar. We are all moving from birth to death. We all have hopes and fears. We are drawn to love, and thus to pain and anger. We struggle to understand our predicament. We are all thrown challenges to overcome as well as sweet unexpected joys.

We can back up to see our common themes and questions by objectively listening to another's story. Or we can develop an expanded perspective by telling our own story as a detached observer. As an example, Brett's parents divorced when he was a young teen. He remembers a childhood with parents who thrived on social activism. "After the divorce, we lived with my mom. I would write my father letters weekly, even daily. He wrote me twice during my entire childhood. All that he cared about personally and professionally changed," Brett adds. "Where did the father I knew before the divorce go? Who was this man in his place?"

> *If you are confused, there are a thousand differentiations, ten thousand distinctions. If you are enlightened, everything is the same one family.*
>
> — WU-CHIEN

Now as a professional novelist and director, Brett creates rich and complex characters who struggle through relationship and loss of identity. Through his stories he endeavors to better understand the nature of being a male in American society: "Again and again I see men whose lives fall apart, and they don't understand why. It is devastating to witness," Brett explains. "But this is a common story to which I am continually drawn to understand. It holds questions of self-betrayal, the vagrancies of memory, and our hopes of survival."

To cultivate witness consciousness, think about how you would tell a tale of meeting with your opponent. What role are you playing? What conflict makes it compelling? Is there a surprise ending? What twists and turns would rivet you as an observer? What question is being asked?

By sharpening our minds we strive to be clear and ready as we meet our opponents. This is also called the work of the sword. With a quick mental blade we meet the world and engage so we can improve. Sharpening the mind makes us clever, discerning, and potentially deadly. Meanwhile, a true warrior's overarching goal is to serve his or her community, an aim that must not be forgotten. Caring for others, not only will we protect them from abuse, but we will save ourselves when we do not engage our hearts, the power that comes with this sword can be misused needlessly and harm all involved. In the next chapter we will explore the practices of opening the heart and the seeming paradoxes of selfish selflessness and becoming fearless through terror, stronger in vulnerability, and calmer through confusion.

> *You are never really playing against an opponent. You are playing against yourself, your own highest standards. And when you reach your limits, that is real joy.*
>
> — ARTHUR ASHE

CHAPTER SEVEN

# Tune the Heart

*It is life near the bone where it is sweetest.*

— HENRY DAVID THOREAU

*An old story from India tells of a time in the state of Maharashtra where* dacoits *(a class who would rob and murder in gangs) became so bold that they would routinely alert their next victim. One morning a wise and wealthy woman, named Parvatibai, and her husband received word that they would be looted that evening. If they removed anything from the home they would all be killed. The husband decided to gather twenty men to lay in wait for the thieves outside the city. Parvatibai replied that she didn't believe it was worth the unequal fight but bid him well and said she would fight in her own way. She sat quietly and thought most of the morning.*

*Parvatibai then told the servants to prepare a royal meal for fifty that should be ready about midnight. She put on her best sari and took off all her jewelry, save her* mangalasutra, *or wedding necklace. She arranged all the jewelry on a silver tray.*

*About midnight, horse hooves and rattling sabers were heard outside her door. With a gracious smile Parvatibai welcomed into her home the* dacoit *chief, a large smelly man carrying a naked sword. "Come in, my brother, I have been waiting for you and your brothers. Come, eat first before you do your work."*

*The hostess fussed over all the men, making sure that each had eaten their fill. When they were finished she handed the tray of jewelry over to the* dacoit *chief, asking to keep her mangalasutra to assure her husband's long life. The chief, overcome with emotion, replied, "You must keep all your ornaments. You have called me brother and given me a brother's welcome, and we have eaten your salt. We are never unfaithful to those whose salt we eat. You are forevermore my sister, and I will make sure that no one will harm you." With that he told his men to go untie Parvatibai's husband and friends along the roadside. Her house and village were never bothered again.*

Parvatibai demonstrates how a warrior can befriend the fiercest adversary, turning the "other" into one of us. She is first-rate in protecting her family and those in her household without resorting to violence. With a sharp mind, she does not panic, and she creates space for herself when conflict strikes to stay open and creative in her thinking. She also carefully assesses her enemy and her situation with an observing eye. She knows the power of her own environment. For example, she uses the custom of "sharing salt" to her advantage. Best of all, she smartly uses the warrior tool of an open heart, and by respecting her enemy, Parvatibai brings him into her home to create resolution. In this chapter, we will explore these two skills.

> *The best way to knock the chip off your neighbor's shoulder is to pat him on the back.*
>
> — UNKNOWN

I have often noticed, when I state that cultures around the world prescribe that we respect our enemies, that I am misunderstood. These traditions are not saying that you have to like your enemies or that you be stupidly nice to them so they can destroy you. Buddhist author Pema Chödrön would call this interpretation "idiot compassion." Rather, we strive to understand our opponents and to hold them in high regard. We wisely regard their potential, which can be used to help or to destroy us. Also, we regard their equal and worthy position as our opponent. This attitude is not only kind but also an effective way to protect ourselves. Our heads need our hearts engaged, so our words and actions do not cause unneeded harm. Intellect and compassion both serve as a check and balance for the other.

In this chapter we will investigate how to condition our hearts to be resources under stress. We will learn how to stay open to our opponents, to loss, and to our limitations. Since anger closes our hearts and limits our capabilities, here we will also explore how to manage this emotion and stay connected to our humanity.

## Learning from Thou

Over the years NBA basketball coach Phil Jackson has taught his players never to take joy in vanquishing the opponent. Jackson would fine any player that shot three-pointers at the end of the game when there was more than a twenty-point lead. After studying the Lakota's definition of the warrior and teamwork, he explained the attitude of a basketball warrior as "an approach that honors the humanity of both sides while recognizing that only one victor can emerge. A blueprint for giving your all out of respect, not hatred, of the enemy. And, most of all, a wide-angle view of competition that encompasses both opponents as partners in the dance."

> *When love and skill work together, expect a masterpiece.*
>
> — JOHN RUSKIN

Jackson's view reflects his belief in the importance of appreciating and respecting our adversaries. We open our hearts to see them as our equals. In the story above, Parvatibai intelligently treats the *dacoits* as her most honored guests. When we adopt this attitude, we move from a place of separation to an understanding of the cocreated relationship we have with our adversaries. Twentieth-century Jewish philosopher Martin Buber says that when we appreciate our mutual dependence and worth, we move into an "I-Thou" relationship. Our adversary then becomes our equal in every way.

In contrast, often we adopt an "I-it" approach in which the "other" is simply someone who helps me to succeed. You are an object, something that might serve me, or something I will simply toss away. I don't see your value beyond being a resource to be used. We are separate and not equal.

> *In short, we have learned how to dominate people as* things, *but when relating to people as people we still tread wearily in the Dark Ages.*
>
> — GERRY SPENCE

We choose between "I-Thou" and "I-it" relationships every day. Where an "I-it" relationship might be appropriate for when we are grabbing a paper towel, obviously your best friend deserves an "I-Thou" approach. It is Buber's philosophy that when confronting our enemies — and all people — we should uphold the "I-Thou" vision. In fact, many spiritual traditions hold that everything on this earth — the trees, the animals, and water — should be approached with an "I-Thou" attitude.

This perhaps sounds overly altruistic until we look at two studies of the effects of war on Vietnam veterans. Dave Grossman, in *On Killing: The Psychological Cost of Learning to Kill in War and Society*, and Jonathon Shay, in *Achilles in Vietnam*, both found an "intimate connection between the psychological health of the veteran and the respect he feels for those he fought." Those who expressed admiration for the Vietnamese culture and had not created a dehumanizing distance from their enemies, for example, "appeared to be leading happy and productive postwar lives."

*Compassion means that if I see my friend and enemy in equal need, I shall help them both equally.*

— MECHTILD OF MAGDEBURG

In contrast, by adopting an attitude of the enemy as subhuman we actually put ourselves in a precarious position. In *The Warriors: Reflections of Men in Battle*, J. Glenn Gray explains, "This image of the enemy as beast lessens even the satisfaction in destruction, for there is no proper regard for the worth of the object destroyed.... No aesthetic reconciliation with one's fate as a warrior [is] likely because no moral purgation [is] possible."

Sam Keen, in *Faces of the Enemy*, explains that it is when we create an "I-it" relationship with a hated enemy that the worst horrors of war are created. When we can objectify, dehumanize, and destroy the other without guilt, we can commit the most terrible atrocities. Keen contrasts this approach with the heroic tradition where "warrior and enemy form a relationship of mutual respect, compassion, and even admiration.... Heroic warfare gives us our most humanized face of the enemy." In other words, in honoring our enemy, we hold on to our own humanity.

Respect and reverence are not forms of expressing love. We are not talking about "idiot compassion" here. Rather, we create safe boundaries and recognize the potential of our opponent. We know when to say no. You appreciate your enemy *as your enemy*, who can and may wish to destroy you. You don't have to like him or her, but you do recognize that your opponent, however horrible, is your equivalent, if not in strength, at least in importance. Remember the statement "We hold these truths to be self-evident, that all men are created equal"?

This approach is also self-serving, since as you value others, they bring important information to the table and can become potential supporters in your cause. I am no longer alone in my pursuits and in relationship; there is a possibility of a better cocreated solution. The "I-Thou" principle makes us into worthy warriors. There is an African saying "Never give a sword to a man who can't dance." If we don't know how to dance in the cocreated tango described by Jackson, we find ourselves in deep trouble as individuals and as a society. We miss the joy of relationship, we destroy indiscriminately, and we suffer the personal and societal consequences.

The "I-Thou" attitude does not necessarily contain an underlying assumption of nonviolence. Sometimes killing is the natural response in a reverent relationship to alleviate suffering. Gandhi, who strove to hold to an "I-Thou" vision in his interactions with all beings, once said in *All Men Are Brothers*, "I see that there is an instinctive horror of killing living beings under any circumstances whatever. For instance, an alternative has been suggested in the shape of confining even rabid dogs in a certain place and allowing them to die a slow death. Now, my idea of compassion makes this thing impossible for me. I cannot for a moment bear to see a dog, or for that matter any other living being, helplessly suffering the torture of a slow death... I should kill a dog similarly situated because in its case I am without a remedy."

> *He that is of a merry heart hath a continual feast.*
>
> — PROVERBS 15:15

When destruction is warranted, it is critical to be conscious of *how* it is done. Speaking of maintaining the "I-Thou" relationship, litigator Gerry Spence, a native of Wyoming who grew up hunting, explained, "It is in the courtroom that I hunt and kill, and for the killing to be right, it must be done cleanly, without unnecessary wounding, done with respect, done without waste, done without pleasure. And if the killing is done right, and for the right reasons, the killing, too, is right."

## Letting Go to Learn

Striking in Parvatibai's story is her bold willingness to risk her life and give away her prized possessions to save her husband, symbolized in her wedding necklace. She trusts that in *sacrifice* she might find ultimate safety. We see this same understanding in the actions of Yun Ok and Gawain the Good as they bravely offer their own lives to save the men they love and admire. We allow our hearts to be touched, to feel pain, so that we may become stronger and more compassionate.

> *The hero-deed is a continuous shattering of the crystallizations of the moment. . . . Briefly: the ogre-tyrant is the champion of the prodigious fact, the hero the champion of creative life.*
>
> — JOSEPH CAMPBELL

The word *sacrifice* is too tied to religious imagery to resonate in our daily lives, but I use it here specifically to remind us that "giving away to gain enlightenment" has been prescribed as an important practice throughout history. To be a warrior or a leader, we must be willing to let go to learn.

The *learning process* hidden in each conflict has four stages:

1. *Disruption*: I realize I have a problem and try to solve it using what I already know.
2. *Chaos*: I am then pushed to surrender in some way.
3. *Creativity*: I open myself to new possibilities and begin to learn.
4. *Stability*: I apply the learning in a new solution.

We are inclined to try to make our opponents go away and look for a quick fix in the first stage, disruption. To learn, however, we follow the path beyond the disruption and move through chaos, creativity, and back to stability. There we find innovative solutions to reducing the crisis or moving beyond the difficulty. Our enemies may even become our allies. Through learning we find increased awareness and peace.

I cannot learn *anything*, however, unless in the second, chaotic, stage of conflict I am willing to surrender *something*. I might need to release a belief that I have all the answers. Or I might sacrifice my "need to know." As Zen master Suzuki Roshi once said, "In the beginner's mind, there are many possibilities, but in the expert's there are few." When an expert achieves a black belt in the martial arts, she is told that she is now just beginning. It's hard to teach old dogs new tricks, but the secret to not becoming an old dog is the willingness to die daily and be reborn a puppy.

> *When solving problems, dig at the roots instead of just hacking at the leaves.*
>
> — ANTHONY J. D'ANGELO

The chaos stage is dark, confusing, and associated with death. In this second stage we must be willing to die to who we were, even in a small way, so that a new being can emerge. However, the loss of control can cause fear and grief. We may become depressed or numb.

The spiritual traditions teach the importance of letting go through voluntary fasting, short-term celibacy, and release of possessions. We give up pleasures for a time to practice standing strong in adversity. Self-imposed sacrifice seems crazy in our abundant lifestyle, but it does gird the warrior for battles ahead. Through detaching ourselves from things, we find increased freedom. In India to prepare women to let go of their children when they reach adulthood, a guru visits a home and asks the mother to consider giving him her most beloved piece of jewelry when he returns in a week. In the act of giving, the mother practices for the harder loss ahead.

In suffering we recognize the few essential things we hold most dear, those things for which we are willing to risk all else. We then can reprioritize what truly matters to us. But this knowledge also brings terror, since we know that ultimately we will face the loss even of these gems.

> *Some offer wealth; others offer sense restraint and suffering. Some take vows and offer knowledge and study of the scriptures; and some make the offering of meditation. . . . All these understand the meaning of service and will be cleansed of their impurities.*
>
> — BHAGAVAD GITA 4:26–27

Robi Damelin, through suffering the loss of her son to a Palestinian sniper, explains how she found freedom: "I have faced the worst and can now bear anything. After a few minutes of preparation, I can now stand in front of 60,000 people and speak strongly about reconciliation between Israel and Palestine. I am doing what I should have been doing all along."

Warriors also voluntarily use sacrifice to expand their compassion. When we don't eat, we feel the pain of the hungry in the world. When we give away financial security, we can open ourselves to the struggles of the poor. At midlife, to learn how to live the next half of our lives more fully we often struggle and find new tenderness for others. When my son went off to high school and I turned forty, I found that I had held very tightly to a belief that I was a "young mother just beginning the parenting journey." With that prized possession, I didn't have to think about mortality, or whether I was spending enough time with my children, since I thought I had plenty of time to squander.

It took some suffering before I was able to sacrifice my "young mother" belief and face the inherent sorrow of motherhood. I had to say good-bye to my own youth and accept where I now stood. I was very sad, even depressed, as I let go of the first half of life. For this very reluctant midlife warrior, it wasn't a voluntary sacrifice. Yet my son went to high school and started to plan for college, and I withdrew from my friendships and family. To save my relationships with my children and husband, which would be my symbolic *mangalasutra*, I had to create the tray of the beliefs that I had once held dear and open the door to face my own midlife thieves.

And as I suffered the loss I realized that I wasn't alone. I found the grief of any mother who has deeply loved her children and must then let them go. I understood a tiny bit better the terrible misery of parents who lose their children to war and disease. I ached for those who can see the end of their lives and doubt if they spent their time well. My heart cracked open, and in the cracking, I was afforded a more sweeping view of life. In weakness I was strengthened. It is only in this open, tender place that I have ever truly learned compassion.

> *When you get extremely soft, then you become hard and strong.*
>
> — THE TAI CHI CLASSICS

Since we don't often practice sacrifice and voluntary suffering, we are often unequipped to handle the pain that comes with being alive. Even with the wonderful health and comfort that Western culture provides, we are paradoxically fragile. Just as with the other skills of the warrior, facing suffering takes practice. What sacrifices might you make to better understand your children, your employees, or your opponents? How can you strengthen yourself to handle loss with bravery and grace?

There are so many temporary escapes from suffering: drinking, shopping, working, writing, eating, reading, doing drugs, having sex — and the list continues. Yet only through the warrior's work of letting go and feeling the sorrow that comes can we find ultimate relief from our pain. It can be terribly hard, and we must be as brave as Parvatibai, but it is worth it. "Many wanted me to take antidepressants after my sister was killed," said Nadwa Sarandah. "But I refused. I have to have the feelings to have the power to do something." When running we become stuck in the same dark place.

> *Those who do not know how to weep with their whole heart don't know how to laugh either.*
>
> — GOLDA MEIR

When we hand over our prized possessions we find that everything transforms. Ironically, our tray is often returned with treasures untouched and accompanied by new gifts and protection that we never could have imagined. Thomas Moore, in *Dark Nights of the Soul*, provides no illusions that we might ever rise from the dark place of chaos. Some terrible event, like the death of a loved one, divorce, or illness may make us question whether living is worth the suffering. Yet in this pain, he counsels, lies the true richness of life. It is here where we find surprising truth, beauty, and art. It is here also where we find our essential selves. We become reborn into who we truly are and are energized to raise our sword once again.

## Working with Time and Doing Our Part

We accept both our losses and the resulting emotions to forge a connection with our hearts. To hold onto this connection, and the accompanying peace, it helps to acknowledge that we each are playing a small but absolutely critical part in the ongoing story of humankind. We seem to believe that if we just commit, our problems will be resolved within a few hours or, in international conflicts, under a year. When they are not, these conflicts are called "unresolvable" and our opponents "impossible," and we give up as though we only have one shot. Yet professional athletes play a lot of games before they become champions. In the meantime, they engage with opponents repeatedly and with respect so that they can play some more. The conflict isn't really over, even when the season is done, and that's okay. There is warrior wisdom in this recognition that we must simply do our part in the greater evolution of our communities. As we accept how much time we have, we also accept our commonality and the equal importance of each of us; we each have a role to play, and play we must.

Essentially, conflict takes time. If we look for the beginnings of the Israeli-Palestinian conflict, we go back in history hundreds of years. I am working on conflicts today that I realize started when I was ten years old. Rosemary Partridge, author and minister, describes this as "the long body of Time." I believe that each conflict has a stabilizing solution waiting at its completion. However, when that completion might be is anyone's guess. Perhaps the parties find themselves better served by prolonging turmoil. In the meantime, we will struggle forward as long as a few can hold a vision of peace as their purpose. We are on the road to resolution but often blind to where we are in the journey, and therefore we believe we are lost and that there are no answers.

> *The arc of history is long, but it bends toward justice.*
>
> — DR. MARTIN LUTHER KING JR.

Recently I was reading about the Irish peacemakers who brought their country to the Good Friday agreement after hundreds of years of strife. The beginnings of the *agreement* alone began fifty years before the final signing in Northern Ireland on Good Friday 1998. Within that fifty-year period, peace activists from both the Ulster Defence Association and Sinn Fein saw themselves laboring toward reconciliation through continued bombings, assassinations, and prison terms. The process was anything but neat and smooth. Instead, a few, plagued with constant doubts and witness to the continuous parade of caskets holding their comrades and fathers, shared a common dream. To the negotiation table for the Good Friday agreement, the leader of the small Alliance Party, Lord Alderdice, brought his three children. He is quoted as saying, "If we don't reach the Promised Land until the next generation, so be it. Somebody has to work in the desert." When the agreement had been signed, Monica McWilliams, leader of the Northern Ireland Women's Coalition, burst into her home to tell her two sons the good news. Her eight-year-old asked, "Mom, does that mean all the murders will stop?" McWilliams replied, "No, unfortunately, it doesn't.... We've made a deal and now we're going to have to build it and building is going to be harder than making it." And still the brave Irish warriors' work continues.

> *Let us not talk of karma, but simply of responsibility toward the whole world.*
>
> — HIS HOLINESS THE DALAI LAMA

A friend who had practiced martial arts for many years met a young man at the door of her *dojo* (studio) who was coming for the first time. The young man asked, "When is the course over?" My friend smiled wisely and replied, "It is never over." The young man never came back.

Focusing on the future when I will win, when I will be able to say "I did it," creates an unhappy individual and an unbalanced warrior. Focusing on doing my part and serving the greater good brings inner peace. By tuning our heart to the long body of time, we then can engage in a challenge over the long haul, even if we might not see resolution. As Helen Keller once said, "I am only one, but I am still one. I cannot do everything, but still I can do something. And because I cannot do everything I will not refuse to do the something that I can do." Winning doesn't matter nearly as much as playing well, and that is truly the only thing we can control.

## Managing Anger

Throughout this chapter, we have focused on being willing to improve through loss, pain, and even hopelessness. Yet, anger can be the ultimate test for an everyday warrior. My wise friend Phil Heron once told me, "He who gets angry loses, it's that simple." Another wise Phil, the professional basketball coach Phil Jackson, assessed the adversary in the 1990 NBA play-offs in a similar manner: "I realized that anger was the Bulls' real enemy, not the Detroit Pistons. Anger was the restless demon that seized the group mind and kept the players from being fully awake." To keep our hearts and minds active through conflict, we must manage our anger.

> *Do not be quickly provoked in your spirit, for anger resides in the lap of fools.*
>
> — ECCLESIASTES 7:9

Anger distracts us. When it fully takes hold, our survival-based instincts rule and we can lose full access to our creative capabilities. We close our hearts and expose ourselves and others to harm. We will lash out with a quick reaction instead of providing a centered response. In the story above, Parvatibai's husband demonstrates this pitfall as he rushes to capture the *dacoits*.

When angry we often do things that we later regret. "Speak when you are angry, and you will make the best speech you will ever regret," said Civil War writer Ambrose Bierce. Furious, we throw our code of conduct to the floor as we take no prisoners. When the fire cools, only embarrassment and cleanup remain. It feels so good to get angry. I often feel moved by anger's passion to speak my mind and share all my secret thoughts. And I am always sorry later.

> *If you are patient in one moment of anger, you will escape a hundred days of sorrow.*
>
> — CHINESE EPIGRAM

But, you might be asking, isn't anger most needed when we need to conquer an opponent in battle? Ancients and moderns agree that the battle is the worst place of all to bring this emotion to the fore. The three-thousand-year-old Chinese text on conflict, *The Art of War*, is specific about the unneeded loss that is suffered when anger in battle is not controlled: "If the general is not victorious over his anger and sets them swarming like ants, one-third of the officers and soldiers are killed and the walled city not uprooted — this is the calamity of attack." The philosopher Seneca, in his treatise *On Anger*, stated: "But against enemies, it may be said, 'there is need for anger.' Nowhere less. The requirement there is not for impulses to be poured out, but to remain well tuned and responsive. What else leaves the barbarian shattered, for all his greater strength of body and powers of endurance? What else, if not his anger, its own worst enemy? Gladiators too, are protected by skill but left defenseless by anger."

The Japanese text on battle *The Book of Five Rings* is also specific about cultivating a state of clarity beyond anger: "It is imperative to master the principles of the art of war and learn to be unmoved in mind even in the heat of battle."

We don't want to repress anger, or any emotion, for that matter. Instead we want to use its power so that we remain in the driver's seat. Pema Chödrön suggests, "If we're angry when we sit down to meditate, we are instructed to label the thoughts 'thinking' and let them go. There is nothing wrong, nothing harmful, about this underlying energy.... Anger without fixation is none other than clear-seeing wisdom." Dan Millman, in *The Way of the Peaceful Warrior*, explains, "True emotion... is pure energy flowing through the body.... The way to control emotions, then, is to let them flow and let them go." We don't repress the emotion or blast it onto another. Instead, we recognize we are angry, let ourselves be angry, and learn why this anger has come. We let anger "be" but not "do." Below are four suggestions for managing anger so it doesn't control you:

1. *Breathe*. Thich Nhat Hanh, in *Anger: Wisdom for Cooling the Flames*, suggests looking into a mirror, breathing, and smiling at yourself to bring yourself back to the present.
2. *Hesitate*. Seneca suggests, "Hesitation is the best cure for anger... the first blows of anger are heavy, but it waits, it will think again."
3. *Go to gratitude*. Ask yourself, What are five things I am thankful for?
4. *Look for the root*. As Gerry Spence advises when facing anger, "Follow the pain to find the answers."

Our opponents are our equals, and they are worthy of engagement. They expand not only our minds, as we saw in the last chapter, but also our hearts. Through the softening that learning from them provides, we become stronger and more durable. As just one small piece in a great puzzle, we remember that we are here to serve, and in the struggle we find a greater peace. Allowing our emotions to be and to flow responsibly from our hearts keeps us centered and more protected.

> *The fly cannot be driven away by getting angry at it.*
>
> — AFRICAN PROVERB

People who bother or disgust us can place great tests on both our intellect and our heart. As they attack our beliefs and ignite our emotions, we need to use all the skills discussed so far — engaging, sharpening our minds, and tuning our hearts — to deal with the unique challenges they present. As we will explore in the next chapter, an everyday warrior can apply some additional special techniques to learn from these trickiest of adversaries.

CHAPTER EIGHT

# Learn from the People Who Drive You Crazy

*One's own self is well hidden from one's own self:*
*of all mines of treasure, one's own is the last to be dug up.*

— FRIEDRICH NIETZSCHE

A simple scenario: You are asked to convince a small group of financial executives to fund a new project. When you begin to present your case, one of the execs, Dan, quickly interrupts: "I don't think you've considered this thoroughly. I don't believe your data." You try to smile politely and explain your conclusions. As you push through your presentation, you become flustered as Dan yawns and looks at his calendar. Soon other executives look at their watches, and one goes so far as to open a newspaper. Dan snaps, "What else do you have?" Your throat tightens as you say, "Not much, I apologize," and stammer through a summary. You barely remember the last five minutes as the misery of defeat sets in. You hate Dan and all that he stands for. "What a rude, self-centered, and ruthless creep! Why would I want to work with that bunch of unaware dolts?" you think, leaving the conference room, "What an idiot

I am." Then you spend the next month reliving that meeting in your mind and hating Dan. Welcome to crazy-making captivity — you have just been taken hostage.

Dealing with tough opponents like Dan requires special skills above and beyond what we have learned. In this final chapter we explore five different techniques to recognize and address adversaries that drive us especially nuts. They might be jealous, selfish, irresponsible, or mean. Maybe they are rude, disrespectful, cruel, or arrogant. Depending on their behavior, we may pity them, speak ill of their actions, or be completely disgusted and unwilling to be in their presence. Regardless of our response to them, the people who make us crazy have a hold on us, which can sometimes feel like a vice.

These adversaries give us windows into our childhood. In my home you can probably guess by the list above that "rude" and "disrespectful" were not traits that I was expected to develop into my adulthood. However, we cannot give away our traits; the best that anyone can do is hide something like "rude" and "disrespectful" in a dark, internal closet. And you can't lock those closet doors either, so those traits find ways to get out from time to time. Since we haven't spent much time with them, and when we did, we knew we were doing something "bad," these traits are scary, awful surprises. They are appalling and worrisome when we meet them in another, like in Dan, and they are horrid to find in ourselves.

When those traits, or our *shadows*, appear, we go to a fight-flight-freeze response. The deeper buried our shadow, the more destructive or delusional we become. So when "rude" and "disrespectful" push on us from the outside, our first inclination is either to run or to freeze, illustrated in the scenario above as a complete loss of confidence and blanking out, or to "attack," which could appear as a future character assassination of Dan. When I start insulting another and swearing for good measure, I know I am in shadow territory! My heart closes, and compassion disappears.

We sometimes try to destroy this evil enemy with whatever methods we have at our disposal. Many prominent therapists, including C. G. Jung, Sam Keen, and Robert Johnson ascribe the worst atrocities of human civilization to fear and running from our own shadow. We see in others what we have rejected in ourselves. We make them into the devil/enemy and set out to destroy them. We all have the capacity to commit atrocities in our homes, communities, and businesses. Sadly, the casualties in everyday life are often those we love most, like our children, siblings, and ourselves.

> *It is surely better to know that your worst enemy is right there in your own heart.*
>
> — C. G. JUNG

There is another way to approach these disowned parts. Instead of seeing them as "bad" or "evil," we can view those closeted pieces as traits that if owned and developed can bring us great benefit. "Disrespectful," for example, was a critical tool in the civil rights movement. Nonviolent activists publicly disagreed with those who believed in segregation. All protest is a form of disrespect. There may be times when you might want to bring disrespect out of the closet and take it for a spin.

For the remainder of this chapter, we will first use a multipart exercise and explore four alternative approaches to make peace with our crazy makers. As we have done with other types of opponents, we first identify our adversary and our internal roadblocks. Then we will engage to release the wrestling hold that crazy makers have on us. Select the engagement strategy that best fits you, depending on your individual style.

## Identifying the Inner Opponent

As Søren Kierkegaard once said, "An unconscious relationship is more powerful than a conscious one." Or said a bit differently, what we repress controls us. If "rude" troubles me, I am not going to fight against it very well. Without a conscious relationship with this aspect of myself, I am held hostage by it. However, if I am comfortable with my own inner impoliteness, if I know its characteristics and benefits, I will have more fancy moves up my sleeve to bring the meeting back under control. Unafraid of being perceived as offensive, I might stop the presentation in the example above, look Dan in the eye, and ask, "What don't you believe?" or, "I'm confused; I sent you a package of information before the meeting. What brought you here?"

Much has been written on working with the shadow to find inner peace, and I have included a short bibliography if you want to learn more. If a situation becomes more than you might wish to tackle, I would also suggest finding professional support. To identify a crazy-making adversary:

1. When someone bugs you, start by listing all the reasons why. Take advantage of your internal passion (anger) to discover what gets under your skin. No holds barred, write a list that no one will see stating the reasons why the crazy maker is a complete ass and not worth the dirt on your shoes. Be nasty, be honest, let it all out, including those personal things that you wouldn't say in public. For example, "He is rude, mean, and self-centered. Dan is an idiot and a lousy leader," and so on.

   When I was describing this exercise to a friend, he lit up and told me about his childhood journal. In it he had written a piece he called "Mean Dave." It began "Dave is the meanest, dumbest, worst brother in the world," continued to list all the horrible things he believed about his sibling, and ended with "and sometimes he's nice."

2. Ask yourself, How is my identity attacked by this behavior? Or, How does that person take me hostage? What happens within me? Does he or she make me feel unimportant, crazy, or like "an idiot"?
3. Author Ken Wilber calls the next step "responsibility and reversal." Recognize that the only person who can make you feel anything is *you*. Taking responsibility for my emotions means that I am only a victim to myself. The good news is that I can decide if I want to feel more or less stupid after my meeting with Dan. I can also decide whether or not "rude" is going to disgust me. Now *reverse* each statement you wrote down, turning them from absolutes about the other: "He is..." to possibilities about you: "I can be..." Move from "Dan is rude, mean, and self-centered" to "I can be rude, mean, and self-centered." Taking this step can knock all the wind out of your sails as you think, "So, now what do I do? Does this mean that I am the terrible person I suspect I am?"

> *The end of our Way of fencing is to have no fear at all when confronting the inner enemies as well as the outer enemies.*
>
> — TESSHU, NINETEENTH-CENTURY SWORD-MASTER AND TUTOR OF THE MEIJI EMPEROR

If these realizations are intense, the fight-flight-freeze reflex will certainly kick in. We might find ourselves saying, "Well, I will never be rude again.

It is inexcusable, I can't believe I made another feel like I did with Dan. I must be vigilant and never repeat such behavior." Don't go there! This fight for control will only cause larger disasters, and it is this kind of repression that makes holy wars possible. We may also want to run away from the possibility that we could be disrespectful. "That's not a problem," I might decide. "I'll think about these things another day."

## Making Peace

Applying these techniques to the painful sister-in-law, Suzie Politics, from the introduction, first we would list all the things we dislike about her. We hate how Suzie is closed-minded, gets in our face, and is naive and exclusionary of others. She is moralistic, self-satisfied, and blind, and she's following a ridiculous and destructive party line. We feel misunderstood, since she appears to think we are stupid or need to be saved. It is frustrating and maddening. No wonder we don't want to be around her!

So we first recognize that we too have the capacity to be pushy, moralistic, exclusionary, and clueless. This might not be the best news; we are identifying the internal enemy. It might help to pretend that these combined unpleasant traits partially comprise an aspect of you that has not been fully explored. Like the Roman god Janus, these qualities can provide another view into the world that will watch your back and show you what you have been missing. Try on the possibility that this internal presence *has gifts to give you*, but because you didn't like her or his behavior, you have refused to receive them. If you can make peace with this "subpersonality" it will provide new resources.

The Dan or the Suzie on the outside is still a painful person. You don't have to like them or their poor behavior. However, the goal of this exercise is to help you fight better and not be taken hostage by their actions. Once the exercise is completed, it should allow you to creatively and calmly resolve the situation.

> *To mortify and even to injure an opponent, reproach him with the very defect or vice... you feel... in yourself.*
>
> — IVAN TURGENEV

Our subpersonalities can also be understood as *archetypes*, or the universal roles we each play. C. G. Jung, who coined the term, described *archetypes* as symbolic images that, although they might vary in detail, have a basic pattern. For example, we all have the common archetypes described as mother, father, lover, virgin, witch, prophet, hero, and so on within us. Sometimes these roles are described in terms of the Greek gods and goddesses. Some therapists use Hera, Demeter, Zeus, Eros, Persephone, Hades, Hecate, and so forth to explain the pieces of ourselves with which we might be battling.

For instance, our inner child or Persephone is that playful, sweet, innocent being within. She is naive and curious. Persephone delights in beauty and gets distracted by the flowers along the path. A lovely subpersonality to be sure, but she can be "clueless" or "stupid" when it comes to meeting with a fierce opponent. But she can sometimes be our best defense. In folktale after folktale the "fool" always triumphs.

In contrast, our "father" or inner Zeus is strong and clear in his decisions. He watches over the situation and renders fierce judgment. He works with power and has a kingdom to protect. This aspect within can be "heartless" and "cruel" in his verdicts. Yet when clear boundaries and tough decisions are needed, calling on this archetype may be our strongest response.

Some roles I am happy to play and am thrilled to be perceived as. Others, I hide away. However, each has valuable gifts and can be very powerful protectors. Even though some inner archetypes might terrify you, think of them as potentially good. They are on your team; you just haven't asked them to play in the daylight yet. They may have the capacity to destroy and do great harm, but if they are understood and put on the active players list, even these terrifying abilities can save our lives. To make peace we want to:

4. Accept that *any trait you hate can also be good*. Repeat to yourself, "I am rude, I am rude" until it no longer matters. Then ask yourself, What can be good about being rude? In *The Dark Side of the Light Chasers*, Debbie Ford advises that we pretend we are talking to two of the most evolved and accepting people we know (Mother Teresa, Buddha, a beloved grandmother). Ask them, "What gift is in my (rudeness, meanness, impatience)?" Notice the surprising answers! For example, the suffragettes were impatient in their fight for a woman's right to vote. Their actions were also probably considered both rude and unbecoming.

> *Shakyamuni Buddha said, "Judge not others; judge only yourself." What appear to be faults in others may actually be reflections of our own emotional afflictions.*
>
> — GESHE NGAWANG DHARGYEY

In regard to sister-in-law Suzie, we might pretend to ask Thomas Jefferson, since this is about politics, what gifts can be found in moralistic and closed-minded behavior. He might remind us that being closed-minded or firm about equal rights for all formed this country. Everything has its place.

In the next steps we will learn to connect with our internal opponent. We will attempt to *listen* to our problematic subpersonality or the Suzie and Dan within. Jung suggested writing, art, music, and movement as ways to unite with active imagination and learn more about these adversaries. In the following steps you will learn how to write to your shadow. Think of this as a fun experiment. Since my rational mind can find it a bit disconcerting, I tell myself, "Whether or not I am really talking to a subpersonality, it doesn't matter. If this exercise helps, I'll pretend for a bit."

5. Find a quiet spot. Open this sometimes difficult conversation by saying to yourself, "I want to talk to that part within me that can be rude" or, "I want to talk to my inner Suzie."
6. Write, "Who are you?" with your dominant hand. Switch the pen to your nondominant hand and let this subpersonality answer. Or, if you'd rather not write, place a doll or figurine in front of you and pretend it is your inner adversary. (I know this sounds weird, but just give it a try.)
7. Ask your internal teacher how old she is (it helps to know when she might have been sent away), what she looks like, and what she wants you to know, switching between hands, if writing, for questions and answers.
8. He may be nasty, rude, and angry because of your years of inattention, so be prepared for some impasses along the way. I have found I might write, "I hate you for being so stubborn," and receive, "The feeling is mutual." Give this internal player a name, write down what he looks like, and ask him what gift he has to give you.

9. Close out the conversation if it gets too intense, and know that you can return to it again. The five-part sparring process — taking up your shield, opening, engaging, closing, and conditioning — described in chapter 5 applies to internal battles as well as external ones.

Talking to our internal Suzie, we learn that she just wants to do it right. She wants answers that make the world safer. She hates how wishy-washy we can be. Suzie is a fighter. She may actually reflect an aspect of our *inner warrior* or *hero* that we have not yet owned, that will stand behind strong beliefs and protect them. But if we haven't developed these hero traits, they will come out sideways, like they do in our sister-in-law.

We can own this inner hero and choose to turn closed-mindedness into a firm, educated resolve. We can own stubbornness and stand strong when needed. Moralistic behavior can be fostered into discernment and a strong code of ethics.

The Dan within might tell you that a strong, succinct case convinces intellectual opponents. "You want to put forth a compelling argument? Don't waste anyone's time," he might say. "You weren't prepared and didn't understand your audience." The internal Dan can help you recognize all the angles so you can be convincing and confident. Harsh or not, he can protect you.

## Other Engagement Strategies

If you find the above writing exercise to be too time-consuming and cumbersome, here are four alternative peace-making techniques. First, among indigenous cultures, community members use masks and ritual theater to bring out all bothersome aspects and fully experience and develop them. You might wear the mask of the cynic and act out that role to better understand it within yourself. Also, through rites of passage, women learn to accept the role not only of virgin, for example, but also of mother, crone, and even whore.

Each October we have available a form of ritual theater to integrate our disowned parts. For example, a newly divorced young mother, Mandy, confronted her fears of misperception last fall when she chose to be "white trash" single mom for Halloween: "I worked it to the hilt all that night," she said, "and now I can better laugh at my worries about others seeing me in that role."

A second alternative that poet Robert Bly suggests is to make peace by "eating the shadow." In this process, he asks the person onto whom he has projected a disowned trait to give it back to him. For example, if you recognize that a woman is holding your inner witch "go to that woman, greet her cordially, and say, 'I want my witch back.' If she gives it back, then turn to the left, facing the wall, and eat it."

Well, I could envision Bly's full ceremony possibly in a workshop setting, but in day-to-day living it might cause some confusion! So instead, perhaps we can visualize sprinkling a bit of "rude" on our lunches each day until that projected piece no longer holds us captive. Or after a tough exchange with someone who is driving us crazy, we can pretend to "eat the cynic."

A third approach is to perceive our four bodies — physical, emotional, creative, and intellectual — as possible crazy-making internal opponents. (Refer back to chapter 2 for a review of these aspects.) By looking at our adversaries on the outside, we can discover which of our four bodies requires more attention and integration. For example, the rude internal Dan would belong to our physical self that is pushing us to prepare and notice worldly details.

So, if we were taught when we were young not to be wild, we may find that creative folks drive us especially nuts and thus that our creative body has been ignored. Julia, as an example, was raised to be a proper young lady. Her mother told her often not to dance and to calm her unruly black curls. As an adult she was most bothered by those who were uncouth, loud, or inappropriate — aspects of the creative body. As Julia has nurtured her own wild side as an adult, by dancing and exploring her sensual nature, she is not only happier but less rattled by obnoxious behavior.

> *To find a fault is easy; to do better may be difficult.*
>
> — PLUTARCH

A fourth and final practice was inspired by Buddhist and Taoist beliefs about how to alleviate suffering. These traditions teach that we can find peace by accepting life's opposites as equal and necessary parts of the whole. In other words, we need black to have white, there is no up without down, with creativity comes unkempt wildness, and intellect brings impatient brashness. You wish to be compassionate; you must learn about its balance with cruelty. None of these traits work alone. They can all be used wisely, just as the Taoist general employs the thief's skills in chapter 3.

To practice "equanimity," as it is called in Buddhism, and to make some peace with undesirable parts of myself or others, I find it helpful to create a place beyond opposites within me. To make this sanctuary of sorts, first identify a trait you don't like and pair it with its opposite. For example, take rudeness and pair it with politeness. Then visualize holding one trait on your left and the opposing trait on the right, holding the perspective that both are necessary and potentially valuable. Now draw a large imaginary circle around each of the opposing traits and place the almond-shaped intersection around your heart and stomach region.

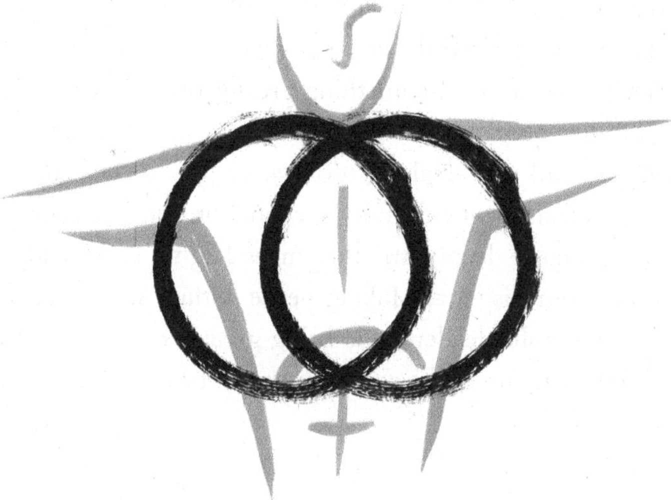

Next focus on this intersecting space sitting at your core. Allow the two traits to fully mix, or dance, with one another. Using our example, you might then understand what polite rudeness or rude politeness might mean. The intersection, or mandorla as it is called, often feels expansive, creative, and more complete. Here you are touching what exists beyond opposites or duality. Many traditions consider the mandorla an opening to infinite possibility and innovative answers. At a minimum, holding this unity for a bit can be a quick calming tool when our buttons are being pushed and we lose perspective.

As Thomas Moore says, "Your purpose in life may be to become more who you are and more engaged with the people and the life around you, to really live your life." As Gawain the Good faces his shadow in the Green Knight, Gawain realizes that he is not just a man of principles but also one who cares about his own corporal survival. His form of peacemaking is to wear the green girdle on his left arm as a symbol of his earthly, dark, and unruly side. Cross-culturally the left hand and the color green are associated with creativity and nature. Gawain becomes a wiser knight through this process and perhaps more compassionate toward the struggles we all face as we try both to survive and to serve something greater than ourselves. Irrational as this practice of shadow work may seem, it may be the most powerful peacemaking tool we've got. If we remember that every trait, be it culturally accepted or not, has a purpose, we can dip more deeply into this mixed bag we carry within us to resolve our disputes. Making peace within, we can become strong, honorable leaders who bring greater resilience, awareness, and harmony to the community and to ourselves.

# Conclusion

*Life does not accommodate you, it shatters you.*
*It is meant to, and it couldn't do it better.*
*Every seed destroys its container*
*or else there would be no fruition.*

— FLORIDA SCOTT-MAXWELL

An old film clip shows aikido's founder Morihei Ueshiba on a rooftop gently turning and guiding a Japanese woman in traditional dress. In the grainy black-and-white image, it appears that Ueshiba and the woman are artfully dancing as an organized pair, but soon one realizes that the master is simply practicing his martial art with the delicate beauty. Ueshiba effortlessly transforms serious self-defense into a soothing ballet.

We may dance with some as friends, and for others we must move back and forth as their opponent. You may even need to be an adversary to those you love, albeit reluctantly a source of your children's, parents', or friends' angst and frustration. Yet conflict and opponents are inevitable. We are each working to survive, to be at peace, and to bring our unique views to the world. Since our beliefs about how to best thrive differ, we will bump into each other, and our views will clash; it comes with the program. I hope though that, with time, my own clumsy bumping and clashing will someday hold a glimmer of Ueshiba's graceful form on that rooftop.

> *The bravest sight in all the world is a man fighting against odds.*
>
> — FRANKLIN K. LANE

As we battle, some opponents take us to our knees or throw us flat on our backs and leave us deeply wounded. "Why get up?" we might think. "If I don't engage, don't love, or don't try, perhaps I won't be hurt again." It's a logical point of view; why would we ever choose to consciously expose ourselves to more anguish?

Yet those I interviewed for this book are compelling individuals precisely because they got back up again. They took a turn on the floor with daunting partners they may not have consciously chosen, and despite the risks and tremendous pain, they brought forth new creativity and magnificence. Psychologist Brendan Pratt, who assists clients to rise again and again to confront learning disabilities, asks a simple question: "Who is the greater hero: Superman or Indiana Jones?" "For me, the answer is clearly Indiana Jones," says Brendan. "Sure, Superman can leap tall buildings in a single bound and bend iron, but he is only afraid of an obscure mineral called kryptonite. Meanwhile, look at Jones; he is deathly afraid of snakes and heights, yet he faces them anyway. Unlike Superman, Indiana Jones is very vulnerable as an average human being, but he continually chooses to confront his fears and overcome his limitations to accomplish his goals. That's hero material."

To rise to meet our challenges, we can apply the book's disciplines not just when meeting individual opponents, but in each moment. We can begin our day with a symbolic "bow" that includes gratitude and recognition that today anything can happen. We can equip ourselves each morning with our shield of ethics and a dose of meditation and self-reflection. Each challenge at work and at home can then become a valuable encounter and an opportunity to learn more, each an avenue for cultivating both our intellect and our compassion. Before we go to sleep at night, we can end as we began by recognizing what has occurred and appreciating what is working in our lives. We can then recover and integrate what we have experienced, so we can rise again and fight tomorrow a bit smarter.

May you continue to heroically face your challengers and "keep dancing." I wish for you the strength and passion to fight the good fights for your family, your company, or for our global community.

> *If you yourself are at peace, then there is at least some peace in the world.*
>
> — THOMAS MERTON

I am constantly amazed at what just one courageous person can do. Kenyan Wangari Maathai, winner of the 2004 Nobel Peace Prize, tells the story that when she was growing up in Nyeri in central Kenya, there was no word for *desert* in her mother tongue, Kikuyu: "Our land was fertile and forested. But today in Nyeri, as in much of Africa and the developing world, water sources have dried up, the soil is parched and unsuitable for growing food, and conflicts over land are common. So it should come as no surprise that I was inspired to plant trees to help meet the basic needs of rural women... to help heal the land and break the cycle of poverty." In the early 1970s Maathai created the Green Belt Movement, which inspired thousands to plant 30 million trees across Kenya. People are paid a small amount for each seedling they grow, giving them an income as well as improving their environment.

This elegant solution to a growing environmental and financial crisis was not without its formidable opponents: "In the 1970s and 1980s, as I was encouraging farmers to plant trees on their land, I also discovered that corrupt government agents were responsible for much of the deforestation by illegally selling off land and trees to well-connected developers," said Ms. Maathai. By the early 1990s, livelihoods, rights, and even many lives in the Rift Valley were lost when people in President Daniel arap Moi's government encouraged Kenyan communities to attack one another. "Mr. Moi's government strongly opposed advocates for democracy and environmental rights; harassment, beatings, death threats, and jail time followed, for me and for many others," she explains.

Yet Maathai's underlying purpose and her warrior nature endured. In 2002, some thirty years after the founding of the Green Belt Movement, Kenyans elected a democratic government, in which Ms. Maathai became the assistant minister for environment and natural resources.

> *A pessimist sees the difficulty in every opportunity; an optimist sees the opportunity in every difficulty.*
>
> — WINSTON CHURCHILL

May we remember, as we fight our battles, Maathai's words as she accepted the Nobel Peace Prize: "To celebrate this award, and the work it recognizes of those around the world, let me recall the words of Gandhi: My life is my message. Also, plant a tree."

And may your everyday warrior work also cultivate change for the better and demonstrate how each of our lives can be a vibrant, courageous message of possibility.

APPENDIX

# Quick Reference to the Four Opponent Types

| | PHYSICAL | EMOTIONAL | CREATIVE | INTELLECTUAL |
|---|---|---|---|---|
| Threatens | Resources or safety | Relationships or feelings | Unique expression | Beliefs and understanding |
| Initial reaction | To problem-solve | To run away | To get frustrated | To feel bugged or to discount |
| Characteristics | Appears to have random impact | Brings messy, hard-to-grasp feelings | Emphasizes a set of rules that may be unspoken | Places view of reality and self in question |
| Some Typical Examples | Natural elements<br><br>Illness<br><br>Competitors | People we love<br><br>Threats to our relationships, self-esteem, and things we value | Institutions, governments<br><br>Cultural norms<br><br>Teachers, peers, superiors | Strange cultures<br><br>Opposing ideologies<br><br>Painful people |
| Inner Opponents (chapter 3) | Our wonderful, wacky brains | The fear of loss | Our love of stability | Our unwillingness to face extremes |
| Reap the Rewards (chapter 4) | Clarity | Connection | Strength | Inner Peace |
| Sharpen the Mind (chapter 6) | Cultivating the observing eye | Creating space through meditation | Blending with our opponents | Fostering witness consciousness |
| Tune the Heart (chapter 7) | Learning from Thou | Letting go to learn | Working with time and doing our part | Managing anger |
| Learn from the People Who Drive You Crazy (chapter 8) | | | | Learn from the people who drive you crazy |

# Notes

## Introduction

1 *One must think like a hero* ... May Sarton, *Journal of a Solitude* (New York: Norton, 1992), 101.

2 *In order to have an enemy* ... www.worldofquotes.com.

3 *heroic warriors, as described in the myths of Camelot* ... Chögyam Trungpa, *Shambhala: Sacred Path of the Warrior* (Boston: Shambhala, 1984), 28.

3 *Yet the classical warrior's highest aim* ... Howard Reid and Michael Croucher, *The Way of the Warrior* (New York: Fireside, 1987), 11.

4 *Israeli Robi Damelin and Palestinian Nadwa Sarandah* ... personal interview, Washington, D.C., May 16, 2005.

5 *Hidden blessings* ... Rebecca Wells, *Little Altars Everywhere* (New York: HarperCollins, 2003), xviii.

6 *the dual-faced Roman god, Janus* ... Janus is considered one of the oldest of the Roman gods. Eric Chaline, *The Book of Gods and Goddesses: A Visual Directory of Ancient and Modern Deities* (New York: HarperCollins, 2004), 47.

7 *Nothing would more contribute* ... www.worldofquotes.com.

## Chapter 1. See Your Enemy as a Teacher

11 *Listen to your enemy, for God is talking*... www.wisdomquotes.com.

11 *In India, everything has a purpose*... This common Asian folktale is a *Jataka*, a story that describes the past reincarnations of Buddha. *Jataka* stories offer a moral lesson and are reenacted in Hindu and Buddhist temples or on street corners in India and Nepal. For additional information on *Jataka* tales, see Cheryl Jones and Gowri Parameswaran, "Tales from India," *Book Links* 10, no. 3 (December/January 2000–2001).

13 *If you want to make enemies*... www.wisdomquotes.com.

14 *the etymology of the word enemy*... *Webster's Encyclopedic Unabridged Dictionary of the English Language* (New York: Portland House, 1989), 472.

14 *information that we most need at this time*... *opponents as potential teachers*... Brian Swimme and Thomas Berry, *The Universe Story: From the Primordial Flaring Forth to the Ecozoic Era: A Celebration of the Unfolding of the Cosmos* (San Francisco: HarperCollins, 1992), 133.

14 *Be grateful even for hardship*... Morihei Ueshiba, *The Art of Peace*, compiled and translated by John Stevens (Boston: Shambhala, 1992), 86.

15 *is a Jataka*... Jones and Parameswaran, "Tales from India."

15 *Without up there is no down. Without black, we have no white*... Alan Watts, *The Book* (New York: Vintage, 1989), 14.

15 *A newly married Iraqi woman*... personal interview, Washington, D.C., May 20, 2005. For more information on assisting women and children in war-torn countries including Iraq, visit Women for Women's website, www.womenforwomen.org, or call (202) 737-7705.

16 *Jerry White, cofounder and president*... Jerry White, *Landmine Survivors Network Annual Report 2004* (Washington, D.C.: www.landminesurvivors.org), 1.

17 *Whenever we demonize*... Matthew Fox, *Sins of the Spirit, Blessings of the Flesh: Lessons for Transforming Evil in Soul and Society* (New York: Harmony, 1999), 343.

17 *destruction is rarely our best or only available response*... Sun Tzu, *The Art of War: A New Translation*, translated, essay, and commentary by the Demna Translation Group (Boston: Shambhala, 2001), 9.

17 *the beginning of the Bhagavad Gita*... Mohandas K. Gandhi, *The Bhagavad Gita According to Gandhi* (Berkeley: Berkeley Hills Books, 2000), 36–43, 60–61.

18 *When we are faced with an enemy*... His Holiness the Dalai Lama and Nicholas Vreeland, *An Open Heart: Practicing Compassion in Everyday Life* (New York: Black Bay Books, 2002), 21.
18 *However, if we seek to minimize injury*... Sun Tzu, *Art of War*, xvi.
18 *Quantum physicists view the universe*... Margaret J. Wheatley, *Leadership and the New Science* (San Francisco: Berret-Koehler, 1992), 11–12.
18 *Hindu texts similarly use the analogy*... Watts, *The Book*, 16, 19.

## Chapter 2. Identify the Threat

22 *Once upon a time, goes a legend*... This tale comes from the Nanai people of the Amur River in the far east region of what is now Russia. *Nanai* means "people of this place," and their historical roots trace back to this region for thousands of years. (www.traveleastrussia.com/nanai.html). Other versions of the Beldy story are captured by Aaron Shep on his website www.aaronshep.com/stories/index.html as "The Twins Go to War" and in Dmitri Nagishkin, *Folktales of the Amur: Stories from the Russian Far East*, "How the Beldys Stopped Fighting," translated by Emily Lehrman (New York: Abrams, 1980), 193–98. Twins are a cross-cultural symbol of marrying the opposites or of deep reconciliation.
23 *four aspects are defined*... Deidre Combs, *The Way of Conflict: Elemental Wisdom for Resolving Disputes and Transcending Differences* (Novato, CA: New World Library, 2004), 12–15.
26 *Yet complex systems, like people*... Wheatley, *Leadership*, 125.
26 *their individual rhythms and patterns*... Wheatley, *Leadership*, 124–30.
27 *a powerful sense of "knowing our opponent" emerges*... Malcolm Gladwell, *Blink: The Power of Thinking without Thinking* (New York: Little Brown, 2005), 3–8.
28 *bouncing electrons and neutrons*... Fritoj Capra, *The Tao of Physics: An Exploration of the Parallels between Modern Physics and Eastern Mysticism* (Boston: Shambhala, 1999), 81.
28 *we develop default styles based on our past preferences*... Combs, *Way of Conflict*, 7–15.
28 *then you must change interrogators"*... Michael Bond, "The Interrogation Room: Inside the Minds of an Israeli interrogator and a

Palestinian prisoner," *Utne Reader*, issue 128, (March-April 2005), 38.

29 *When we are panicked, our brain stem*... Dan Baker, *What Happy People Know: How the New Science of Happiness Can Change Your Life for the Better* (New York: Rodale, 2003), 80, and John J. Ratey, *A User's Guide to the Brain: Perception, Attention and the Four Theatres of the Brain* (New York: Vintage, 2001), 171–72.

29 *threats feel like things*... Thomas Lewis, Fari Amini, and Richard Lannon, *A General Theory of Love* (New York: Vintage, 2000), 32.

30 *These intellectual constructs*... see Ratey's discussion on convergence zones, *User's Guide to the Brain*, 187.

30 *emotions are a critical part*... Lewis, Amini, and Lannon, *General Theory of Love*, 70.

31 *The limbic, or "old mammalian," brain*... Lewis, Amini, and Lannon, *General Theory of Love*, 25, 39, 40.

31 *three to five times more likely*... Lewis, Amini, and Lannon, *General Theory of Love*, 62, 80.

31 *"Connectedness assures survival"*... Lewis, Amini, and Lannon, *General Theory of Love*, 149.

32 *child will monitor the facial expressions*... Lewis, Amini, and Lannon, *General Theory of Love*, 61.

33 *It takes some degree of fearlessness*... Trungpa, *Shambhala*, 28.

33 *Tung-shan was asked*... Thomas Cleary, ed., *Teachings of Zen* (Boston: Shambhala, 1998), 47.

34 *As free human beings*... Quoted in Mary Craig, ed., *The Pocket Dalai Lama* (Boston: Shambhala, 2002), 57.

35 *This brain, and the prefrontal lobes*... Lewis, Amini, and Lannon, *General Theory of Love*, 27, and Joseph Chilton Pearce, *The Biology of Transcendence: A Blueprint for the Human Spirit* (Rochester, VT: Park Street Press, 2002), 26, 41, 43.

36 *studying not only the hearts but also the laws of India*... Keshavan Nair, *A Higher Standard of Leadership: Lessons from the Life of Gandhi* (San Francisco: Berret-Koehler, 1997), 84–85.

37 *There is no other task but to know your own original face*... Cleary, *Teachings of Zen*, 32.

39 *threaten existing structures*... Walter Truett Anderson, *Reality Isn't What It Used to Be: Theatrical Politics, Ready-to-Wear Religion, Global Myths, Primitive Chic, and Other Wonders of the Postmodern World* (San Francisco: HarperCollins, 1990), 249–50.

39 *In sparring with a partner*... Rick Fields, ed., *The Awakened Warrior: Living with Courage, Compassion, and Discipline* (New York: Tarcher/Putnam, 1994), 119.

40 *Peter Block describes how we*... Peter Block, *The Answer to How Is Yes: Acting on What Matters* (San Francisco: Berret-Koehler, 2003), 1–3.

52 *A traditional Sufi tale*... James Fadiman and Robert Frager, eds., *Essential Sufism* (San Francisco: HarperCollins, 1997), 134.

## Chapter 3. Meet Your Inner Opponents

53 *Don't cling to your own understanding*... Quoted in Thomas Cleary, ed., *The Pocket Zen Reader* (Boston: Shambhala, 1999), 200.

53 *This is a story of another tiger*... Adapted from http://folkloreandmyth.netfirms.com/tibet.html.

55 *Recently I awoke to a radio*... Morning Edition, National Public Radio, November 16, 2004; *Bozeman Chronicle*, November 16, 2004.

57 *When we are startled*... John J. Ratey, *A User's Guide to the Brain: Perception, Attention and the Four Theatres of the Brain* (New York: Vintage, 2001), 312.

58 *Our focus moves from "we" to "I"*... Thomas Lewis, Fari Amini, and Richard Lannon, *A General Theory of Love* (New York: Vintage, 2000), 23, 26.

58 *"In this war, morality*... Quoted in Tzvetan Todorov, *Facing the Extreme: Moral Life in Concentration Camps*, translated by Arthur Denner and Abigail Pollak (New York: Holt, 1997) 31–32.

58 *Whatever a rival*... Glenn Wallis, trans., *The Dhammapada: Verses on the Way* (New York: Modern Library, 2004), 118.

59 *Come near my children*... Lewis, Amini, and Lannon, *General Theory of Love*, 25–26.

59 *"Father and son... hungry together*... Todorov, *Facing the Extreme*, 35.

59 *Better a patient man*... Quoted in Maggie Oman Shannon, *One God, Shared Hope: Twenty Threads Shared by Judaism, Christianity, and Islam* (Boston: Red Wheel, 2003), 112.

59 *the prefrontal lobes*... Ratey, *User's Guide to the Brain*, 230.

59 *The short route (the "low road")*... Ratey, *User's Guide to the Brain*, 172–73, 234.

60 *O Lord, remember not only the men and women* . . . Quoted in Maggie Oman Shannon, *Prayers for Healing: 365 Blessings, Poems, and Meditations from Around the World* (Berkeley: Conari Press, 2000), 221–22.

60 *our basic mental health* . . . Shannon E. French, *The Code of the Warrior* (Lanham: Rowman & Littlefield, 2003), 4.

60 *neural pathways* . . . Lewis, Amini, and Lannon, *General Theory of Love*, 56, 132–38, and K. C. Cole, *Mind Over Matter: Conversations with the Cosmos* (New York: Harcourt, 2003), 216–17.

61 *If a man should conquer in battle* . . . William Wray, *Sayings of the Buddha: Reflections for Every Day* (London: Arcturus, 2004).

61 *Since the 1970s Elizabeth Loftus* . . . Ratey, *User's Guide to the Brain*, 183.

61 *"If an emotion is sufficiently powerful* . . . Lewis, Amini, and Lannon, *General Theory of Love*, 130.

61 *Our memories are also malleable* . . . Ratey, *User's Guide to the Brain*, 186–87.

63 *Knowing others is intelligence* . . . Quoted in Shannon, *Prayers for Healing*, 258.

64 *"Befriend death* . . . conversation with Patrick O'Neill, October 23, 2003, "Thresholds of Collective Wisdom" retreat, Minneapolis, Minnesota.

67 *It's a human being* . . . Quoted in Mitch Horowitz, "Taking the Third Side," *Science of Mind* 78, no. 2 (February 2005), 86.

67 *In 1971 C. P. Ellis and Ann Atwater* . . . Osha Gray Davidson, *The Best of Enemies: Race and Redemption in the New South* (New York: Scribner's, 1996), 187.

68 *In the initial steering committee* . . . Davidson, *Best of Enemies*, 253.

68 *"We were asked to meet to plan* . . . interview with Amy Goodman, *Democracy Now*, National Public Radio, July 4, 1997.

68 *As they planned the conference* . . . Davidson, *Best of Enemies*, 267, 275–76.

69 *By the end of the ten days* . . . interview with Amy Goodman, and Davidson, *Best of Enemies*, 283–85.

69 *"I used to think that Ann* . . . Quoted in Davidson, *Best of Enemies*, 285.

70 *"What is a highway to one is disaster to the other* . . . Jelaluddin Rumi, *The Essential Rumi*, translated by Coleman Barks with John

Moyne, A. J. Arberry, and Reynold Nicholson (San Francisco: HarperCollins, 1995), 30.

70 *that the Devil as a personified*... Elaine Pagels, *The Origin of Satan* (New York: Random House, 1995), xvi.

70 *The Hebrew term satan*... Pagels, *Origin of Satan*, 39.

70 *"As literary scholar Neil Forsyth says of the satan*... Pagels, *Origin of Satan*, 30.

71 *In the Book of Job*... Pagels, *Origin of Satan*, 41.

71 *It wasn't until the Gospel of Mark*... Pagels, *Origin of Satan*, xvii, 61.

71 *we now find aberrations*... Pagels, *Origin of Satan*, 182.

71 *in Tibetan Buddhism demons*... Connie Zweig and Steven Wolf, *Romancing the Shadow: A Guide to Soul Work for a Vital, Authentic Life* (New York: Ballantine, 1997), 53.

71 *In the Hindu tradition*... Zweig and Wolf, *Romancing the Shadow*, 53.

71 *From the Taoist*... Kakuzo Okakura, *The Book of Tea* (Tokyo: Kodansha, 1989), 64, 65.

71 *Perceiving one's own group*... Pagels, *Origin of Satan*, xix.

71 *"the use of Satan*... Pagels, *Origin of Satan*, xix.

72 *What is hateful to yourself*... Quoted in Maggie Oman Shannon, *One God, Shared Hope: Twenty Threads Shared by Judaism, Christianity, and Islam* (Boston: Red Wheel, 2003), 72.

72 *is not human or of God*... Pagels, *Origin of Satan*, 184.

72 *demonize the Jew, who did not see Jesus as*... Pagels, *Origin of Satan*, 27, 65, 104.

72 *supported the wider acceptance*... Pagels, *Origin of Satan*, 64, 65.

72 *C. P. Ellis found his*... Davidson, *Best of Enemies*, 112.

72 *Returning to the lessons of Auschwitz*... Todorov, *Facing the Extreme*, 122, 123, 230, 231.

73 *As Primo Levi states*... Todorov, *Facing the Extreme*, 123.

73 *"circle of humanity."*... Todorov, *Facing the Extreme*, 230–31.

## Chapter 4. Reap the Rewards

75 *In China, a well-known thief was conscripted into the military*... This is an adaptation of an old Chinese story attributed to Taoist philosopher Liu An. A version of this tale can also be found in Benjamin Hoff's *The Tao of Pooh* (New York: HarperCollins, 1983), 59–60.

77 *subdue the other's military without battle*... Sun Tzu, *The Art of War: A New Translation*, translated, essay, and commentary by the Demna Translation Group (Boston: Shambhala, 2001), 84.

77 *Everyone has a spirit that can be refined*... Morihei Ueshiba, *The Art of Peace*, compiled and translated by John Stevens (Boston: Shambhala, 1992), 13.

78 *"It is in moments of extreme duress*... José Saramago, *All the Names* (New York: Harvest, 2001), 201–02.

78 *there is a story in the East*... Chögyam Trungpa, *Shambhala: Sacred Path of the Warrior* (Boston: Shambhala, 1984), 25.

78 *This path draws heavily from Buddhism*... Howard Reid and Michael Croucher, *The Way of the Warrior* (New York: Fireside, 1987), 26–27.

78 *Japanese samurai*... Rick Fields, ed., *The Awakened Warrior: Living with Courage, Compassion, and Discipline* (New York: Tarcher/Putnam, 1994), 3.

79 *Life is so generous*... Fra Giovanni, quoted in Maggie Oman Shannon, *Prayers for Healing: 365 Blessings, Poems, and Meditations from Around the World* (Berkeley: Conari Press, 2000), 92.

82 *"In our [Muslim] ritual*... Azim Khamisa, "A Father's Journey to Forgiveness: How I Healed from the Slaying of My Son," *Science of Mind* 77, no. 3 (March 2004), 84. For more information on Khamisa's work see, Azim Khamisa and Carl Goldman, *Azim's Bardo: A Father's Journey from Murder to Forgiveness* (Scotts Valley, CA: Rising Star, 1998).

82 *"I would help my country protect all its children*... Khamisa, "A Father's Journey," 85.

83 *"He dearly loved his grandson*... Khamisa, "A Father's Journey," 86.

83 *"Our goal is to create*... Khamisa, "A Father's Journey," 86.

83 *As expert surfer and doctor Mark Renneker remarks*... Quoted in the movie *Riding Giants*, directed by Stacy Peralta, 2004.

84 *only two emotions, love and fear*... Gerald Jampolsky, *Good-Bye to Guilt: Releasing Fear through Forgiveness* (New York: Bantam 1985), 4, and Dan Baker, *What Happy People Know: How the New Science of Happiness Can Change Your Life for the Better* (New York: Rodale, 2003), 80.

84 *"Everybody loves something...* Quoted in Pema Chödrön, *The Places That Scare You: A Guide to Fearlessness in Difficult Times* (Boston: Shambhala, 2002), 4.

85 *What keeps us alive...* Quoted in Kenyatta Monroe-Sinkler, "Daily Guides to Richer Living," *Science of Mind* 78, no. 2 (February 2005), 46.

85 *Eve Ensler...* Quoted in Nina Utne, "Heartland," *Utne Reader* issue 127 (January-February 2005), 8.

88 *"As soldiers we were taught to fill our backpacks...* Phone conversation with Duncan Grady, January 31, 2002.

88 *Compassion is the ability to feel the pain...* Matthew Fox, *A Spirituality Named Compassion and the Healing of the Global Village: Humpty Dumpty and Us* (San Francisco: HarperCollins, 1990), 2–3.

88 *Nuala O'Faolain, author of...* Nuala O'Faolain, "How to Write Your Memoir, Seven Honest Tips for Best-Selling Success," *Utne Reader*, issue 120 (November-December 2003), 93–94.

89 *"For the warrior...* Trungpa, *Shambhala*, 46.

89 *When the mind sees this...* Ajahn Chah, "Bodhinyana," quoted in Jeff Schmidt, ed., *365 Buddha: Daily Meditations* (New York: Tarcher/Putnam, 2002), 1.

90 *I was born when all I once feared...* Rabia, quoted in Kenyatta Monroe-Sinkler, "Daily Guides to Richer Living," *Science of Mind* 78, no. 2 (February 2005), 62.

91 *On the path of service...* Ram Dass and Paul Gorman, *How Can I Help? Stories and Reflection on Service* (New York: Knopf, 1985), 225.

91 *"The ideal of...* Trungpa, *Shambhala*, 50.

95 *founder of aikido...* Fields, *Awakened Warrior*, 137.

96 *What the warrior renounces...* Trungpa, *Shambhala*, 65.

97 *"For the true warrior, there is no warfare...* Trungpa, *Shambhala*, 64.

97 *This being human is a guesthouse...* Jelaluddin Rumi, *The Essential Rumi*, translated by Coleman Barks with John Moyne, A. J. Arberry, and Reynold Nicholson (San Francisco: HarperCollins, 1995), 109.

99 *called The September Project...* For more information on this international program, visit www.septemberproject.org.

99 *And so in groups...* Ralph Waldo Emerson, quoted in "Taking the Third Side," *Science of Mind* 78, no. 2, (February 2005), 89.

100 *With malice toward none, with charity for all*... Quoted in Maggie Oman Shannon, *Prayers for Healing: 365 Blessings, Poems, and Meditations from Around the World* (Berkeley: Conari Press, 2000), 39.

## Chapter 5. Engage

101 *A monk asked, "If on the road*... Quoted in Josh Bartok, ed., *Daily Wisdom: 365 Buddhist Inspirations* (Somerville, MA: Wisdom Publications, 2001), 217.

103 *A knowledge of the path*... Quoted in Jim Palmer, comp., *Big Wisdom (Little Book): 1,001 Proverbs, Adages, and Precepts to Help You Live a Better Life* (New York: W Publishing Group, 2005), 46.

103 *This is a story from the kingdom of Camelot*... This tale was likely written in the fourteenth century by an unknown author who was sometimes called the "Pearl-poet." Much critique has been written on this famous tale. For more information see *The Complete Works of the Pearl Poet*, ed. Casey Finch (Berkeley and Los Angeles: University of California Press, 1993), Derek Brewer and Jonathon Gibson, *Companion to the Gawain-poet* (Rochester, NY: D. S. Brewer, 1997), and the following two websites: www.sparknotes.com/lit/gawain/index and www.luminarium.org/medlit/gawain.

107 *The martial arts also codify*... Sun Tzu, *The Art of War: A New Translation*, translated, essay, and commentary by the Demna Translation Group (Boston: Shambhala, 2001), 82–89.

107 *The purpose of discipline*... Henry Miller, quoted in Sy Safransky, *Sunbeams: A Book of Quotations* (Berkeley: North Atlantic Books, 1990), 93.

108 *"not only how he should interact*... Shannon E. French, *The Code of the Warrior* (Lanham, MD: Rowman & Littlefield, 2003), 3.

108 *Similarly, Joseph Campbell describes*... Joseph Campbell, *Masks of God: Oriental Mythology* (New York: Penguin, 1991), 505.

108 *And from the Lakota tradition*... Quoted in Maggie Oman Shannon, *Prayers for Healing: 365 Blessings, Poems, and Meditations from Around the World* (Berkeley: Conari Press, 2000), 18.

109 *Model Rules of Professional Conduct*... see www.abanet.org for American Bar Association rules for attorneys and www.ama-assn.org for the American Medical Association's ethical rules for physicians.

109 *Why do we need a code?*...French, *Code of the Warrior*, 3, 14.
109 *our code protects us*...French, *Code of the Warrior*, 241.
109 *"The code of a warrior is*...conversation with Phil Heron, Bozeman, Montana, February 16, 2005.
110 *Without their shield*...French, *Code of the Warrior*, 4, and Jonathon Shay, *Achilles in Vietnam: Combat Trauma and the Undoing of Character* (New York: Scribner's, 1994), xiii.
111 *The Greek Stoics*...French, *Code of the Warrior*, 63–65, 88–89, 144, 156.
112 *To keep internal balance*...Robert A. Johnson, *Owning Your Own Shadow: Understanding the Dark Side of the Psyche* (San Francisco: HarperCollins, 1991), 19, 27.
113 *I have never in my life*...Dudley Field Malone, quoted in Palmer, *Big Wisdom*, 169.
113 *The haka*...www.newzealand.com/travel/about-nz/culture/haka-feature/haka.cfm.
113 *"The Chickpea to the Cook"*...Jelaluddin Rumi, *The Essential Rumi*, translated by Coleman Barks with John Moyne, A. J. Arberry, and Reynold Nicholson (San Francisco: HarperCollins, 1995), 132–33.
115 *"Don't kid yourself"*...Conversation with Phil Heron, Bozeman, Montana, February 16, 2005.
116 *This kind of gratitude might seem solely altruistic*...Dan Baker, *What Happy People Know: How the New Science of Happiness Can Change Your Life for the Better* (New York: Rodale, 2003), 81.
116 *Another helpful attitude to incorporate*...Mohandas K. Gandhi, *The Bhagavad Gita According to Gandhi* (Berkeley: Berkeley Hills Books, 2000), 217–18.
116 *We can learn even from our enemies*...Ovid, quoted in Palmer, *Big Wisdom*, 312.
118 *Excellence is an art*...Quoted in Kenyatta Monroe-Sinkler, "Daily Guides to Richer Living," *Science of Mind* 78, no. 2 (February 2005), 47.
118 *Use these four guidelines while you fight*...Deidre Combs, *The Way of Conflict: Elemental Wisdom for Resolving Disputes and Transcending Differences* (Novato, CA: New World Library, 2004), 34.
120 *The Massachusetts-based nonprofit Stop It Now!*...Quoted in Joan Tabachnick, "Dialogue Breaks New Ground," *The Crime Victims Report*, vol. 8, no. 5, December 2004, 65–66.

120 *One female survivor*... Gayle McNab, quoted in "Consultation on Restorative Justice and Violence Against Women, February 8 and 9, 2001" (Prepared for the Department of Justice, Saskatchewan, The Law Foundation, compiled by Saskatoon Community Mediation Services June 26, 2001), 8.

120 *A recovering sex offender*... Quoted in Joan Tabachnick, "Dialogue Breaks New Ground," *The Crime Victims Report*, vol. 8, no. 5, December 2004, 65–66.

120 *If we could read the secret history*... Henry Wadsworth Longfellow, quoted in Safransky, *Sunbeams*, 19.

120 *Dialogue is*... David Bohm, *On Dialogue* (New York: Routledge, 1996), 11, and William Isaacs, *Dialogue and the Art of Thinking Together* (New York: Doubleday, 1999), 11.

121 *Now there is cure in coolness and calm*... Jeff Schmidt, *365 Buddha: Daily Meditations* (New York: Tarcher/Putnam, 2002), 84.

121 *"cool inquiry,"*... Peter Senge, *Fifth Discipline Fieldbook: Strategies and Tools for Building a Learning Organization* (New York: Doubleday, 1994), 360.

122 *The Palestinian/Israeli group the Parent's Circle*... Nick Taylor, "Peace on the Line," *Guardian Unlimited*, 12 May 2004). Available at www.guardian.co.uk/prius/parttwo/story/0,14195,1214886,00.html.

123 *"There are always stories*... Nadwa Sarandah, presentation at All Souls Church, Washington, D.C. on May 17, 2005.

123 *has logged over 530,000 calls*... Robi Damelin, presentation at All Souls Church, Washington, D.C., May 17, 2005.

123 *"The greatest mistake we made was to allow*... Quoted in Taylor, "Peace on the Line."

123 *A man who is swayed by passions*... Carol Tavris, *Anger: The Misunderstood Emotion* (New York: Touchstone, 1989), 31.

123 *Once the dialogue starts*... Taylor, "Peace on the Line."

123 *His Holiness the Dalai Lama also sees dialogue*... Quoted in Mary Craig, ed., *The Pocket Dalai Lama* (Boston: Shambhala, 2002), 102.

126 *In researching Vietnam veterans*... Shay, *Achilles in Vietnam*, 187–92.

126 *Anthropologist Angeles Arrien*... Angeles Arrien, *Change, Conflict and Resolution from a Cross-Cultural Perspective* (Sausalito, CA: Angeles Arrien, audiocassette, 1991).

127 *I've always said*... www.wisdomquotes.com.

128 *"Narrative can transform involuntary*... Shay, *Achilles in Vietnam*, 192.

128 *However, simple narrative in some cases*... Justine Willis Toms interview with Belleruth Naparstek, New Dimensions Radio Program, 2005, program number 3068.

128 *In 1987 Dr. Francine Shapiro pioneered*... Francine Shapiro, *EMDR: Eye Movement Desensitization and Reprocessing: Basic Principles, Protocols and Procedures* (New York: Gilford Press, 2001), 9, 10.

128 *A simple closing exercise that seems*... Shapiro, *EMDR*, 284.

128 *Stretch your arms*... Jelaluddin Rumi, *The Essential Rumi*, translated by Coleman Barks with John Moyne, A. J. Arberry, and Reynold Nicholson (San Francisco: HarperCollins, 1995), 205.

130 *"Physical and mental exercise*... John J. Ratey, *A User's Guide to the Brain: Perception, Attention, and the Four Theaters of the Brain* (New York: Vintage, 2001), 356.

130 *Exercise increases*... Ratey, 359–61, 370, 189.

131 *I can like my fellow men*... Carlos Castaneda, quoted in Sam Keen, "A Path with a Heart: Interview with Carlos Castaneda," *The Awakened Warrior: Living with Courage, Compassion, and Discipline*, ed. Rick Fields (New York: Tarcher/Putnam, 1994), 16.

132 *The Tibetan Shambhala tradition*... Quoted in Matthew Fox, *One River, Many Wells: Wisdom Springing from Global Faiths* (New York: Putnam, 2000), 414.

132 *Becoming Real*... Hugh Prather, *Notes to Myself: My Struggle to Become a Person* (New York: Bantam, 1970), backmatter.

## Chapter 6: Sharpen the Mind

133 *I thank God*... Quoted in Maggie Oman Shannon, *Prayers for Healing: 365 Blessings, Poems, and Meditations from Around the World* (Berkeley: Conari Press, 2000), 123.

133 *From Korea comes a story about a young woman*... This story is accorded its origins in both Korea and in Ethiopia, where the tiger is a lion and the young woman seeks to win over her stepson or a new disinterested husband. Versions of this tale can be found in Joanna Cole, ed., "The Tiger's Whisker," *Best-Loved Folktales of the World* (New York: Doubleday, 1982), 558–60, and Nancy

Raines Day, *The Lion's Whiskers: An Ethiopian Folktale*, illustrated by Ann Grifalconi (New York: Scholastic, 1995).

135 *In comparison, to heighten awareness*... Miyamoto Musashi, *The Book of Five Rings*, translated by Thomas Cleary (Boston: Shambhala, 2000), 19.

136 *As we cultivate an observing eye*... Margaret J. Wheatley, *Leadership and the New Science* (San Francisco: Berret-Koehler, 1992), 82.

136 *We must be courageous to observe*... Quoted in Jill Rosenfield, "Here's an Idea!" *Fast Company* 33 (April 2000), 97.

137 *"Extra use means extra cortex*... Ratey, 60.

138 *"Assumptions will come up*... David Bohm, *On Dialogue* (New York: Routledge, 1996), 23–24.

138 *"Truth can only*... Kakuzo Okakura, *The Book of Tea* (Tokyo: Kodansha, 1989), 68.

138 *Meanwhile, we are wired*... Daniel Goleman, *Emotional Intelligence* (New York: Bantam, 1997), 16–17.

139 *As Einstein once said*... K. C. Cole, *Mind Over Matter: Conversations with the Cosmos* (New York: Harcourt, 2003), 216.

139 *"run out of space, run out of gas*... Ratey, *User's Guide to the Brain*, 62.

139 *Wisdom comes out in*... From "Five Houses of Zen," quoted in Jeff Schmidt, ed., *365 Buddha: Daily Meditations* (New York: Tarcher/Putnam, 2002), 339.

140 *Studies have shown*... Ratey, *User's Guide to the Brain*, 376.

140 *Meditation also appears to boost our immunity*... Joel Stein, "Just Say Om," *Time* (August 4, 2003), 55, and James Shreeve, "Paths to the Mind Brain Link," *National Geographic* 207, no. 3 (March 2005), 31.

140 *At the E. M. Keck Laboratory*... Daniel Goleman, "The Lama in the Lab," *Shambhala Sun* 11, no. 4 (March 2003), 64–72.

140 *Meditation is a process of lightening up*... Quoted in "On Meditation," *Shambhala Sun* 11, no. 4 (March 2003), 57.

142 *Keep your spine straight*... Sakyong Mipham Rinpoche, "Sitting Meditation, Step by Step," *Shambhala Sun* 11, no. 4 (March 2003), 48, 49.

144 *"Merging with your opponent is not a metaphor*... Conversation with Phil Heron, Bozeman, Montana, February 16, 2005.

144 *To practice blending*... Tom Crum, *The Magic of Conflict: Turning a Life of Work into a Work of Art* (New York: Simon & Schuster, 1987), 89.

146 *The Buddhist tradition teaches tong len*... His Holiness the Dalai Lama and Howard C. Cutler, *The Art of Happiness: A Handbook*

*for Living* (New York: Penguin, 1998), 125, and Pema Chödrön, *The Places That Scare You: A Guide to Fearlessness in Difficult Times* (Boston: Shambhala, 2002), 55–60.

146 *Author and lecturer Tara Brach practices "radical acceptance"*... Tara Brach, *Radical Acceptance: Embracing Your Life with the Heart of a Buddha* (New York: Bantam, 2003), 74–79.

148 *our adversaries obstruct our path*... Elaine Pagels, *The Origin of Satan* (New York: Random House, 1995), 39, and James Fadiman and Robert Frager, eds., *Essential Sufism* (San Francisco: HarperCollins, 1997), 235–36.

148 *Another way we can view this*... Deidre Combs, *The Way of Conflict: Elemental Wisdom for Resolving Disputes and Transcending Differences* (Novato, CA: New World Library, 2004), 131–33.

148 *Be patient toward all*... Rainer Maria Rilke, *Letters to a Young Poet* (New York: Vintage, 1986), 34.

149 *looking at ourselves from above*... Ronald D. Davis, Eldon M. Braun, *The Gift of Dyslexia: Why Some of the Smartest People Can't Read and How They Can Learn* (New York: Perigree, 1997), 131.

149 *When a man realizes*... Thomas Byrom, *The Heart of Awareness: A Translation of the Ashtavakra Gita* (Boston: Shambhala, 1990), 60.

149 *In Romancing the Shadow*... Connie Zweig and Steven Wolf, *Romancing the Shadow: A Guide to Soul Work for a Vital, Authentic Life* (New York: Ballantine, 1997), 309.

152 *"Ma'heo'o Great One, Holy Mystery*... excerpted from a prayer written by Henrietta Mann, Martin Luther King Jr. march and rally, Bozeman, Montana, January 16, 2005.

152 *A man cannot be too careful*... www.worldofquotes.com.

153 *Out of Supreme love*... Quoted in Andrew Harvey, *Teachings of the Hindu Mystics* (Boston: Shambhala, 2001), 68.

154 *If you are confused*... Quoted in Cleary, ed., *Teachings of Zen*, 145.

154 *This is called the work of the*... Angeles Arrien, *The Tarot Handbook: Practical Applications of Ancient Visual Symbols* (London: Diamond Books, 1995), 105–14.

## Chapter 7. Tune the Heart

157 *It is life near the bone*... Henry David Thoreau, quoted in Sy Safransky, *Sunbeams: A Book of Quotations* (Berkeley: North Atlantic Books, 1990), 18.

157 *An old story from India*...Adapted from Kathleen Ragan, ed., foreword by Jane Yolen, *Fearless Girls, Wise Women and Beloved Sisters: Heroines in Folktales from Around the World* (New York: Norton, 1998), 170–72.

159 *"idiot compassion"*...Pema Chödrön, *The Places That Scare You: A Guide to Fearlessness in Difficult Times* (Boston: Shambhala, 2002), 77.

159 *Over the years NBA basketball coach*...Phil Jackson, *Sacred Hoops* (New York: Hyperion, 1995), 136.

160 *"I-Thou" relationship*...Martin Buber, *I and Thou* (New York: Free Press, 1971), 56.

160 *In short, we have learned how to dominate*...Gerry Spence, *How to Argue and Win Every Time* (New York: St. Martins, 1995), 2.

160 *We choose between "I-Thou"*...Buber, *I and Thou*, 141.

160 *Vietnam Veterans... "intimate connection between*...Shannon E. French, *The Code of the Warrior* (Lanham, MD: Rowman & Littlefield, 2003), 5–6.

161 *For equality gives strength*...Quoted in *Prayers for Healing*, 129.

161 *"This image of the enemy*...Quoted in French, *Code of the Warrior*, 6.

161 *"warrior and enemy*...Sam Keen, *Faces of the Enemy: Reflections of the Hostile Imagination* (San Francisco: Harper and Row, 1986), 67–69.

161 *"We hold these truths to*...Declaration of Independence, available on www.ushistory.org/declaration/document.

162 *"Never give a sword to a man*...Madronna Holden, "Fierce Music," *Parabola* 27, no. 4 (Winter 2002), 22.

162 *"I see that there is*...Mahatma Gandhi, *All Men Are Brothers: Autobiographical Reflections* (New York: Continuum, 1994), 84.

162 *hunt and kill*...Gerry Spence, *The Making of a Country Lawyer* (New York: St. Martins, 1996), 99.

163 *The hero-deed is a continuous*...Quoted in Joseph Campbell, "The Hero as Warrior," *The Awakened Warrior: Living with Courage, Compassion, and Discipline*, ed. Rick Fields (New York: Tarcher/Putnam, 1994), 66.

163 *The learning process*...Deidre Combs, *The Way of Conflict: Elemental Wisdom for Resolving Disputes and Transcending Differences* (Novato, CA: New World Library, 2004), 62–67.

164 *"In the beginner's mind...* Chödrön, *Places That Scare You*, 1.

165 *In India to prepare...* Joseph Campbell, with Bill Moyers, *Power of Myth* (New York: Doubleday, 1988), 256–57.

165 *Some offer wealth...* Eknath Easwaran, trans., *The Bhagavad Gita* (Berkeley: Nilgiri Press, 1985), 88.

165 *Robi Damelin...* interview, Washington, D.C., May 16, 2005.

166 *When you get extremely soft...* Quoted in Fields, *Awakened Warrior*, 118.

167 *Nadwa Sarandah...* personal interview, Washington, D.C., May 16, 2005.

167 *provides no illusions...* Thomas Moore, *Dark Nights of the Soul: A Guide to Finding Your Way Through Life's Ordeals* (New York: Gotham, 2004), xvi, xix.

168 *Irish peacemakers... Profiles in Courage for Our Time*, introduction and edited by Caroline Kennedy (New York: Hyperion, 2002), 232–46.

169 *Let us not talk of karma...* Quoted in Bartok, *Daily Wisdom*, 295.

170 *"He who gets angry...* Conversation with Phil Heron, Bozeman, Montana, December 7, 2004.

170 *Another wise Phil...* Phil Jackson, *Sacred Hoops* (New York: Hyperion, 1995), 131.

170 *Do not be quickly provoked...* Quoted in Maggie Oman Shannon, *One God, Shared Hope: Twenty Threads Shared by Judaism, Christianity, and Islam* (Boston: Red Wheel, 2003), 92.

170 *"Speak when you are angry...* Tom Carr, *Creative Strategies for Reaching Children with Anger Problems* (Chapin, SC: Educational Media Corporation, 2001), 131.

171 *"If the general...* Sun Tzu, *The Art of War: A New Translation*, translated, essay, and commentary by the Demna Translation Group (Boston: Shambhala, 2001), 10.

171 *"But against enemies...* John M. Cooper (editor), J. F. Procopé (editor), Raymond Geuss (series editor), Quentin Skinner (series editor), *Seneca: Moral and Political Essays* (Cambridge: Cambridge University Press, 1995), 28, 29.

171 *Japanese text on battle...* Miyamoto Musashi, *The Book of Five Rings*, translated by Thomas Cleary (Boston: Shambhala, 2000), 18.

171 *"If we're angry when we sit down...* Chödrön, *Places That Scare You*, 28, 29.

171 *"True emotion*...Dan Millman, *The Way of the Peaceful Warrior* (Novato, CA: H. J. Kramer, 1984), 113.

172 *looking into a mirror*...Thich Nhat Hanh, *Anger: Wisdom for Cooling the Flames* (New York: Riverhead, 2001), 26, 27.

172 *"Hesitation is the best cure for anger*...Tavris, *Anger*, 31.

172 *"Follow the pain*...Spence, *How to Argue*, 69.

## Chapter 8: Learn from the People Who Drive You Crazy

175 *One's own self is well hidden*...Quoted in Sy Safransky, *Sunbeams: A Book of Quotations* (Berkeley: North Atlantic Books, 1990), 26.

177 *It is surely better to know*...Quoted in C. G. Jung, "The Fight with the Shadow," *The Awakened Warrior: Living with Courage, Compassion, and Discipline*, ed. Rick Fields (New York: Tarcher/Putnam, 1994), 235.

178 *"An unconscious relationship is*...Quoted in Pagels, xx.

179 *Author Ken Wilber*...Ken Wilber, "Taking Responsibility for Your Shadow," *Meeting the Shadow*, ed. Connie Zweig and Jeremiah Abrams (New York: Tarcher/Putnam, 1991), 275.

179 *The end of our Way*...Quoted in Fields, *Awakened Warrior*, 121.

180 *pretend that these combined unpleasant traits*...Debbie Ford, *The Dark Side of the Light Chasers: Reclaiming Your Power, Creativity, Brilliance, and Dreams* (New York: Riverhead, 1998), 103.

181 *To mortify*...www.worldofquotes.com.

181 *Our subpersonalities can also be understood as*...Joseph Campbell, *Man and His Symbols* (New York: Doubleday, 1964), 67, 68.

181 *Some therapists use Hera, Demeter*...Jean Shinoda Bolen, *Goddesses in Everywoman: Powerful Archetypes in Women's Lives* (New York: Perennial, 2004), 14–15.

182 *Accept that any trait you hate*...Ford, *Dark Side of the Light Chasers*, 104–6.

182 *Shakyamuni Buddha said*...Josh Bartok, ed., *Daily Wisdom: 365 Buddhist Inspirations* (Somerville, MA: Wisdom Publications, 2001), 327.

183 *writing, art*...Barbara Hannah, "Learning Active Imagination," *Meeting the Shadow*, 296.

184 *First, among indigenous cultures*...Conversation with Angeles Arrien, Paulden, Arizona, October 22, 1997.

185 *"eating the shadow."*... Robert Bly, "Eating the Shadow," in *Meeting the Shadow*, 279.

187 *As Thomas Moore says*... Thomas Moore, *Dark Nights of the Soul: A Guide to Finding Your Way Through Life's Ordeals* (New York: Gotham, 2004), xiv.

## Conclusion

189 *Life does not accommodate you, it shatters you*... Florida Scott-Maxwell, *The Measure of My Days* (New York: Penguin, 1979), 65.

190 *"Who is the greater hero*... conversation with Brendan Pratt, June 3, 2005.

190 *The bravest sight in all the world*... Quoted in Jim Palmer, comp., *Big Wisdom, Little Book* (Nashville: W Publishing Group, 2005), 53.

191 *Kenyan Wangari Maathai*... Wangari Maathai, "Trees for Democracy," *New York Times Late Edition*, December 10, 2004.

192 *A pessimist sees the difficulty*... Quoted in Palmer, *Big Wisdom, Little Book*, 258.

# Selected Bibliography and Resources

## Meditation

Brach, Tara. *Radical Acceptance: Embracing Your Life with the Heart of a Buddha.* New York: Bantam, 2003.
Chödrön, Pema. *The Wisdom of No Escape and the Path of Loving Kindness.* Boston: Shambhala, 2001.
Easwaran, Eknath. *Meditation: A Simple 8-Point Program for Translating Spiritual Ideals into Daily Life.* Berkeley, CA: Nilgiri, 1991.
Harvey, Andrew. *The Direct Path: Creating a Journey to the Divine Using the World's Mystical Traditions.* New York: Broadway, 2000.
Trungpa, Chögyam. *Shambhala: Sacred Path of the Warrior.* Boston: Shambhala, 1984.
Wiley, Eleanor, and Maggie Oman Shannon. *A String and a Prayer: How to Make and Use Prayer Beads.* Boston: Red Wheel/Weiser, 2002.

## Brain Study

Baker, Dan, M.D. *What Happy People Know: How the New Science of Happiness Can Change Your Life for the Better.* New York: Rodale, 2003.

Johnson, Steven. *Mind Wide Open: Your Brain and the Neuroscience of Everyday Life*. New York: Scribner, 2004.

Lewis, Thomas, M.D., Fari Amini, M.D., and Richard Lannon, M.D. *A General Theory of Love*. New York: Vintage, 2000.

Pearce, Joseph Chilton. *The Biology of Transcendence: A Blueprint for the Human Spirit*. Rochester, VT: Park Street Press, 2002.

Ratey, John J., M.D. *A User's Guide to the Brain: Perception, Attention and the Four Theatres of the Brain*. New York: Vintage, 2001.

## Dialogue

Baldwin, Christina. *Calling the Circle: The First and Future Culture*. New York: Bantam, 1998.

Bohm, David. *On Dialogue*. New York: Routledge, 1996.

Isaacs, William. *Dialogue and the Art of Thinking Together*. New York: Doubleday, 1999.

Wheatley, Margaret. *Turning to One Another: Simple Conversations to Restore Hope to the Future*. San Francisco: Berret-Koehler, 2002.

## Shadow Work

Ford, Debbie. *The Dark Side of the Light Chasers: Reclaiming Your Power, Creativity, Brilliance, and Dreams*. New York: Riverhead, 1998.

Johnson, Robert A. *Owning Your Own Shadow: Understanding the Dark Side of the Psyche*. San Francisco: HarperCollins, 1991.

Keen, Sam. *Faces of the Enemy: Reflections of the Hostile Imagination*. San Francisco: Harper and Row, 1986.

Markova, Dawna. *No Enemies Within: A Creative Process for Discovering What's Right about What's Wrong*. Berkeley, CA: Conari, 1994.

Zweig, Connie, and Jeremiah Abrams, eds. *Meeting the Shadow: The Hidden Power of the Dark Side of Human Nature*. New York: Tarcher/Putnam, 1991.

Zweig, Connie, and Steven Wolf. *Romancing the Shadow: A Guide to Soul Work for a Vital, Authentic Life*. New York: Ballantine, 1997.

# Acknowledgments

Books are great opponents in that as I write they teach me not only content, but also how completely surrounded I am by kind and wise souls. I have learned how really good friends like Marcus and Diana Stevens, Phil Heron, Carmen McSpadden, Deborah McAttee, David Baum, and Marilynn Hall can push in just the right manner so that the work and I expand. Craig and Deborah Barber once again provided sage advice and safe space. Sue MacGrath and Jinny and Peter Combs opened their homes and their grand hearts. Editors Jason Gardner and Mimi Kusch added their fantastic expertise and encouragement to help this book take form. I am deeply indebted to all those who shared their stories of bravery and demonstrated how real warriors behave. And to Bruce, without whom nothing would be nearly as right, thank you for your delicious humor, priceless friendship, and wise instruction.

# Index

*Page numbers in italics refer to illustrations.*

# About the Author

Photo by Stenzel Photography

A consultant, speaker, and credentialed mediator, Dr. Deidre Combs coaches individuals and organizations on how to find possibility in conflict. In 1994 she founded Combs & Company, whose diverse corporate, nonprofit, and educational clients include IBM, the Landmine Survivors Network, the U.S. Postal Service, and the U.S. Forest Service. Combs holds bachelor's degrees in mathematics and Spanish from the University of Wisconsin–Madison, a master's from George Washington University, and a doctorate focused in world religions from UCS/Naropa University in Oakland, California. She spent seventeen years in the technology and healthcare sectors as a project manager, software developer, and marketing director. Combs lives in Bozeman, Montana, with her husband and three children. She is the author of *The Way of Conflict: Elemental Wisdom for Resolving Disputes and Transcending Differences*. Her websites are www.wayofconflict.com and www.combsandcompany.com.

# JAICO PUBLISHING HOUSE

Elevate Your Life. Transform Your World.

ESTABLISHED IN 1946, Jaico Publishing House is home to world-transforming authors such as Sri Sri Paramahansa Yogananda, Osho, The Dalai Lama, Sri Sri Ravi Shankar, Sadhguru, Robin Sharma, Deepak Chopra, Jack Canfield, Eknath Easwaran, Devdutt Pattanaik, Khushwant Singh, John Maxwell, Brian Tracy and Stephen Hawking.

Our late founder Mr. Jaman Shah first established Jaico as a book distribution company. Sensing that independence was around the corner, he aptly named his company Jaico ('Jai' means victory in Hindi). In order to service the significant demand for affordable books in a developing nation, Mr. Shah initiated Jaico's own publications. Jaico was India's first publisher of paperback books in the English language.

While self-help, religion and philosophy, mind/body/spirit, and business titles form the cornerstone of our non-fiction list, we publish an exciting range of travel, current affairs, biography, and popular science books as well. Our renewed focus on popular fiction is evident in our new titles by a host of fresh young talent from India and abroad. Jaico's recently established Translations Division translates selected English content into nine regional languages.

In addition to being a publisher and distributor of its own titles, Jaico is a major national distributor of books of leading international and Indian publishers. With its headquarters in Mumbai, Jaico has branches and sales offices in Ahmedabad, Bangalore, Bhopal, Bhubaneswar, Chennai, Delhi, Hyderabad, Kolkata and Lucknow.

SINCE 1946